MEAT LONDON

THE BOOK

by Paul Grout

CLOKE PRESS

For the Roux Family

Foreword

I've concluded, as I get older, that there are three vital components to a happy and fulfilled life: a loving family, good health and a really good, local butcher. And for many years, it was the third of these that was missing for me. Most food you can buy in a supermarket, touring the aisles, peering at varieties of apples, carrots and sourdough loaves. But with supermarket meat, you can't see or smell for sweaty cellophane and packaging; the provenance is generally unclear; and, with every piece ready-cut, the home cook is rendered passive and helpless. Adrift, I struggled for years in London – loved and healthy, but dissatisfied meat-wise. In Yorkshire, where I was a Member of Parliament, my needs were fully met, but in Stoke Newington there was a gaping hole. And then, Meat N16 arrived on Church Street. I can recall quite how my heart leapt as I saw a new sign being erected above the soon to be opened butcher's shop. And I can honestly say that my soaring expectations, all those years ago, have been more than met ever since.

Meat N16 is an oasis of butchering brilliance. For such a tiny shop, the range is huge and the quality second to none. The smell is meaty fresh and the team of butchers are skilled and always cut to order. Beef bones, a turkey crown, eleven chipolatas, onglet, skirt, pork ribs with the membrane removed, no request is ever too much. The staff are friendly, the customer service always caring and thoughtful, and the sausage competition is an annual highlight, with chilli, lemongrass and ginger still my favourite. Not one for unnecessary hyperbole, I can honestly say my trip to Meat N16 is a weekly highlight, combining meat, good health and family all in one. Sunday lunch sorted. A really high quality, healthy cut. And as I stand in the queue, scouring the meat cabinet, I am transported back to holding my Mum's hand – a butcher's daughter herself – as she chose the Sunday joint every Saturday morning in our village butcher's. Family, good health and Meat N16. A beloved trinity.

Ed Balls

CONTENTS

Meat the Butcher: Paul's Story

Everything has to start somewhere. Ideas come to us born out of fun and aspiration, but they have to be developed, nurtured and executed. Well, I'm a butcher not a philosopher but that's how Meat London's first butcher's shop Meat N16 came about.

I started my working life by way of a chef's apprenticeship with the Roux brothers, Chef Albert and Chef Michel. I spent five years in the kitchens of their restaurants while attending Westminster Catering College.

History would dictate that I was not to be the best chef in the industry. I was looking across the stove at a young Marco Pierre White. Gordon Ramsey was on the horizon and Michel Roux Junior was finishing his own apprenticeship in France. The kitchens were full of young people with dedication, natural skills and the belief that they would become the very best. And some of them did! I contributed to the kitchen, but I didn't have the single minded focus or the relentless pursuit of knowledge that those guys possessed.

I was 17 years old when I started at the Roux brothers' Le Gamin' – where I first gutted poultry – and my bosses were very demanding masters. They hadn't yet reached the culinary heights they would later achieve and everything we did was focused on making sure that Roux Restaurants became the very finest restaurants in Britain, probably Europe and possibly the world. Things were either perfect or for the bin. There was no compromise when it came to quality. These were hard times for a young man with no catering background and no idea of the difference between a good carrot and a bad one!

During my 14 years with Chef Albert Roux I was never given a rota with my start and finish time. I was told what time I was expected to be at work, and I turned up. The head chef told me when it was time to go home, and I went. If there was time, the head chef told me to go and eat, so I did.

I was never abused or taken for granted. Both brothers were generous in their praise when things went right and helped their young teams to learn, develop and attain the same standards that they had set themselves and had achieved. The late 1970s and 80s were amazing times in the British restaurant industry and I was extremely fortunate to be riding the crest of the wave at the top table.

When it came time to move to the next restaurant, in order to continue my training and development, I moved to Le Poulbot in Cheapside, my first experience of a Michelin starred restaurant and the first time I ran a 'section' for service. I was then invited to move to Le Gavroche in Lower Sloane Street, a two Michelin star restaurant and the first that the Roux brothers had opened in London. The standard was mind blowing. From there I moved to the Roux Pastry Laboratory on the Wandsworth Road. Chef Michel was one of the finest pastry chefs in the world. In 1976 he was awarded the 'Meilleur Ouvrier de France en Patisserie', an honour that very few achieved. He was a calm, quietly spoken man with unlimited patience for showing his young team how to achieve perfection.

In 1980 the much-coveted letter arrived. The now renowned Le Gavroche needed to move from Lower Sloane Street to Upper Brook Street in Mayfair, so that the restaurant might have a chance of attaining three Michelin star status. I was invited to be part of the team that would move the restaurant and re-open. The Mayfair site was picked for its perfection. The renovation spared no expense or overlooking of the smallest detail. On opening night the room was beautiful, the kitchen was beautiful and the team were primed. Albert Roux had changed up the gears and everything became that bit more intense. And so it came about that in 1981 Le Gavroche became the first restaurant in Britain to achieve three Michelin Stars, and I was part of the team when it happened. It would be highly arrogant to suggest that I played more than a supporting role, but I was there; it was food that I prepared going across the pass, with the head chef's approval.

My apprenticeship finished in 1982 and I wanted a break. Maybe in the back of my mind I had realised that the kitchen wasn't for me. I tentatively approached Chef Albert about the possibility of seeing the restaurant industry from the other side of the pass. I wanted to be a waiter for a while. I was shocked when Chef Albert told me to speak to Le Gavroche's restaurant manager, Mr Silvano Giraldin, an Italian of immense class and stature. I could hardly believe my luck that yet again I would have such an opportunity to learn from the very best. I spent about a year in the 'room' at Le Gavroche. I worked with, and became great friends with Danielle Roux, Chef Albert's

daughter. It was great fun and a real eye opener – my first direct interaction with the customer – but soon enough Mr Roux was in front of me, letting me know that the fun was over and that it was time to come back in the kitchen.

Now my life really would turn in a different direction. The problem with catering college had been the lack of funds and the lack of product to work with. My meat and butchery skills training had been restricted to cutting up a chicken and watching a three-hour demonstration of cutting up a lamb. I asked Chef Albert if I could work on the larder section so that I could learn about meat. Again, Chef Albert didn't hesitate for a second in finding me the best training available. I was packed off to 'Boucherie Lamartine' in Paris, where Monsieur Prosper was deemed to be the best butcher in Paris at that time.

I arrived at Boucherie Lamartine full of confidence. What an opportunity! The shop itself was not big, but, for the first few days, my eyes were agog with the splendour and quality on show. This was a working butcher's shop. It certainly wasn't a dainty Parisian boutique. Every morning the meat would arrive from market and the butchers would begin to cut it into its usable parts, and prepare the shop for the day ahead. From about 7am there would be a steady stream of customers that would continue until closing. Although this was the first of two butcher's shops that would influence my later work, and business model, it was the butchers themselves who remain to this day in my memory. The standard and quality of their work was extraordinary; each of them worked with such speed and deftness. Their skills were on show for everyone to see, and only later would I understand how each of them had such natural ability. They laughed and joked all day, with the customers and each other, and they made time for me. Nothing was too much trouble. Despite having their work to do and despite the regular flow of customers, each of them made every effort to show me, help me or tell me what they could. In truth, they liked to pull my leg. We're talking about butchers here. They enjoyed the opportunity of having a trainee with whom to impart their knowledge and skills, but it was even more fun as they had a young English guy to make fun of. They were happy to entertain me. They invited me to the bars and they invited me to their homes. It was a humbling experience, a generosity of mind and spirit that taught me so much, and remains with me nearly forty years later.

When I returned from Paris, we opened Boucherie Lamartine in Pimlico, London. Primarily the shop was designed to supply the Roux Group with meat, but the retail shop itself was beautiful and took off. The customer base grew and chefs throughout London asked to be supplied. Two years later, Chef Albert was offered the opportunity to take over at John Bailey & Son in Mayfair. The shop had ceased to trade well and the wholesale supply, although reasonable, was in decline. Our business had outgrown the unit in Pimlico and it made good sense to move the wholesale business to Mayfair. We tried to resurrect the shop trade as well. I moved to Mayfair as manager. It wasn't an easy ride, but I was now ordering meat from the farms in England and Scotland, starting to get to know the workings of Smithfield Market in London and ordering directly from suppliers in France. I was learning more and more about the industry and I was still working with some very good butchers. But I'd been with the Roux Group since I had left school and I was getting itchy feet.

I had built good working relationships with some of London's top chefs and the purchasing departments of some of London's top hotels. I forged a good reputation and it was a chef from one of these restaurants who would give me my next opportunity.

I had supplied Simon Hopkinson from since before he opened his first restaurant in Old Brompton Road, South Kensington. Simon was a brilliant cook who loved what he did and was among a small number of chefs who worked directly with their suppliers at a time when many chefs deemed themselves too important to be polite to those who served them. When Simon moved to Bibendum Restaurant I was delighted that he asked me to continue supplying his meat. Apart from his cooking, Simon was a very good teacher and a great many fine chefs seeped into the industry from his kitchen. One of these Chefs was Henry Harris. Henry had been sous chef to Simon and, as Simon, became a very good cook.

It was during a casual telephone conversation with Henry early one morning that I let slip that I was considering my future. Henry seemed a bit taken aback and clarified that I was considering leaving the Roux Group. Within the next day or so Henry was back on the phone telling me about a new and exciting project that he was working on himself. It was a big project that needed a butcher and meat buyer. "Was I interested?"

I was very interested and, after a number of meetings and minimal negotiation, it was with a heavy heart that I decided to leave the Roux Brothers and join the team that was to open the Harvey Nichols Fifth Floor Foodmarket.

Harvey Nichols had been bought in recent years by a Hong Kong-based business man, Mr Dickson Poon, whose stock in trade was luxury brands. The project to open London's finest food market was headed by Dominic Ford, who would feature more in my later life. There was to be a retail market, a wine shop, a café and a restaurant.

I was employed as 'buyer/manager' for the meat and charcuterie departments. I joined a team of three fresh food buyers, a grocery buyer and a wine buyer. On my first day I was introduced to Sue Cloke, who was the cheese and bakery buyer. Sue had worked at Paxton and Whitfield and had developed own label brands for Burberry. Four years after that meeting Sue would become my wife. At Harvey Nichols our first priority was to select our own teams. I was lucky enough to be able to talk two very close friends, and colleagues from previous jobs into joining me. I started with a very good team. My fellow buyers also brought on board some of the top retail talents in London at that time.

We opened in November 1992 with a team of food professionals ready, quite literally, to take on the world. The brief was simple: the Harvey Nichols Foodmarket had to be the best in London. There was no compromise and no expense spared. The owner wanted products that were not available in other outlets. He wanted only the very best available and he wanted us to compete with the other stores on price. Harrods, Selfridges and Fortnum & Mason had years of traditions and experience on us. It was a daunting task, but, without doubt, the first three years at Harvey Nichols were the most fun of my working life. I realised very quickly that it was now my job to set my own standards. Instead of reacting to instruction, I now had to make the decisions, give the instruction and answer for the consequences. At 32 years old, I was full of confidence. Much of what I now did was new to me but Harvey Nichols was a supportive employer; I had people to turn to for whatever I needed.

The direct line manager was a man by the name of Tony Sweet. He came from a butchery background and had a vast knowledge of department store food halls, and how they were supposed to function. Unfortunately, we clashed! Tony was some twenty years older than me and his outlook on butchery and customer service were from a different time. He didn't always agree with my methods and we saw

things from a different view point. I had learnt a lot in France and I saw things from a chef's angle. Traditionally, buyers sat in offices and negotiated with suppliers, but offices were not for us new buyers. We bought food and worked with our teams. We raised eyebrows from the Harvey Nichols hierarchy by making the staff taste the food and eat everything. We worked on the counters teaching the youngsters and meeting the customers. It was an amazing time and I was loving it.

In the early days one or two of the chefs that I had supplied for years asked me to continue to supply them. I proposed the idea of a wholesale meat business and it was agreed by the Board. I had a good friend in the meat business, Barry Gibson, and he worked with me to ensure that I could compete on price with other suppliers. Barry was the main meat supplier at Harvey Nichols and a key asset to what I was doing. Wholesale grew steadily and brought in much-needed revenue to the Foodmarket.

We introduced workshops for customers, events where they could come and listen to suppliers and producers and we hosted customer evenings, sometimes in conjunction with the whole store.

Harvey Nichols gave me so much. I learned about human resources, making margin and how to be a retailer from everyone around me. I went on courses for just about everything. In the end, however, I think Harvey Nichols failed to embrace the culture of young food professionals. It was a department store with no food history and the directors were driving for too much growth; financial investment became more difficult. Cracks starting to show and the Fifth Floor Restaurant never reached potential. As key staff started to move on, there was a reluctance to replace them with the same quality and the business started to tread water.

One day in the mid 90's, a young French girl came into the store to sell saucisson (cured sausage) from Lyon in France – the world capital for charcuterie in my opinion. The girl spoke little or no English but I liked her and I was very interested in the product, so I helped her. Her company had no importer and importing was not our thing. I introduced her to a friend promising that if he imported the product, I would be his first customer. Eventually the deal was done and we all set off to sell the product.

The following year my friend told me that the saucisson was proving very popular and that we had been invited to the factory to witness production and meet the owners. We picked up a car in France, drove to the charcuterie factory and did a tour. The following day we were invited to visit the company's butcher's shop in the local village. This would be the second shop to shape my business life.

The shop was nice, but ordinary – certainly not in the same league as Boucherie Lamartine in Paris. But while we were there a strange thing happened. We were talking to the butcher when an elderly gentleman came into the shop. He all but shouted at the butcher, gesturing with his walking stick, and disappeared through an open door to the side of the shop. The butcher apologised and excused himself for a minute. We all chatted and then curiosity got the better of me. I looked through the open door and there was the butcher cooking a steak on a four-ring gas stove for the old man's lunch. The old man was at a table in the corner with a glass of wine and reading his paper.

That was it! In that split second, my business plan came to me. I wanted a butcher's shop with a restaurant attached. The customers would select their cut and the chef would cook it. One business, encompassing all the professional skills that I had worked for. As soon as I was back to London I committed my idea to paper and I carried it around in my briefcase until 2005.

By the late summer of 2000 I had become disenchanted with Harvey Nichols. I decided, after a little under ten years, it was time to move on.

In the early 2000s Dominic Ford (the Harvey Nichols food and beverage director) also decided it was time for another challenge. By chance one afternoon I met him in a bar and we talked about what we were both doing. I was still touting my business plan and Dominic wanted to set up a restaurant consultancy business. It made great sense to put the two together. Dominic found a financial backer, a business man and farmer by the name of Simon Tindall, and a site in Battersea, south London. The three of us set about opening The Butcher & Grill in the summer of 2006.

The site we took on was a good size and accommodated a retail shop, bar area and restaurant. Dominic did a really good job with the development of the site, and the décor and layout were beautiful. Customers took to the business quickly and the restaurant especially was very busy early on. Simon Tindall wanted us to use his cattle and lambs in the shop and supplied us with some very good product. Slowly the shop was embraced by the locals and the deli part grew very well. The business was all I wanted, and I was having fun at work again. The business, like most, struggled to make money during the early period and it was Simon's generosity that kept the business afloat. We all wanted to expand the business and we agreed to find a second site. Dominic wanted to open in Wimbledon village, but I wasn't convinced as the site was so far from my own home. We found a site in the Village but, again, it didn't suit the retail side of the business and it certainly wasn't to be a Butcher & Grill as per our business

plan. However, in the interest of fair play (democracy and all that) I went along with the idea. Unfortunately, I couldn't love the place and eventually it was obvious that we all wanted different things from the business. We had previously agreed to open a site on Leadenhall Market in the City of London and Dominic and Simon had gone back on the plan. I decided I didn't want to fall out with anyone. I really loved Butcher & Grill (Battersea) and the concept was just as it should be. I was so proud that we had done it. It was never a wrench to walk away. It was, and is, my business model, and it was a great place.

So, I opened by myself in Leadenhall Market in the late autumn of 2009. Big mistake!

My wife has a cheese shop in Leadenhall Market and it was our ambition that I would open a butchery next door. During 2008 the site became available. The two guys who financed my wife's cheese shop made it known that they would like to be involved with my butchery idea. We talked it through and we all agreed on our own financial input. They put up the lion's share of the capital and off we went. The Butcher at Leadenhall opened into the cold of winter and six weeks before Christmas. It wasn't ideal and by Christmas the outside tables and chairs were not bringing the customers that we needed, but we were still less than one financial quarter into the business.

The retail shop did all right, thanks to the Christmas turkey trade, and the general response from the customers was one of excitement that there was a butcher back in Leadenhall Market. After Christmas it was cold. Butcher at Leadenhall was an open unit onto the market's cobbled streets and there was no respite from the cold in the early months. As the warmer weather came towards the end of March so did the customers. They started to understand the concept and liked the idea that they could see their meat being cut and cooked in front of them.

There were two staff who had come with me from Butcher & Grill (Agata Filus and Alisa Adlam) and between us we got the business going. Unfortunately, the early days had put us on the back foot and the financial backers decided they weren't up for the battle. They wanted out.

Agata and I kept the business going for another two years before it all became too much. We had a great summer and the restaurant wholesale business started to grow. The problem with restaurant supply is cash-flow. It takes between six and eight weeks to get paid by restaurants and our suppliers want to be paid on a standard four weeks. It's a tough balancing act. In the end, I was working six full days a week and there was no sign of respite. I looked at the business with the accountants and we concluded that the business could function as a retail/restaurant but not with the wholesale. The head Chef, John Valdes and the manageress, Rosmary Valdes (oddly not related) took on the business.

It's never nice to fail, but the goal posts moved too far from the original vision and it just wasn't going to work. I could just put it all down to a blip on my C.V. but people lost money and it would be disrespectful. I prefer to see it as a lesson and take from it what I can.

While Leadenhall was keeping me awake at night, I received one morning a very strange email:

Hi Paul, I know this is probably the most bizarre email you'll ever get, but do you want to open a business with us? Marc

I knew of Marc Wise through business, but I'm not sure we had ever met. Marc lived in Stoke Newington, and he and his friend, Richard Jocelyn, decided that Stoke Newington Church Street needed a butcher's shop. I was the nominated butcher. Having met Marc and Richard, and talked it through, it was never difficult to make the decision to do it. And so, Meat N16 was born.

BUTCHERY COURSES
here @ MEAT LONDON ...

available courses :

MEAT the SAUSAGE
MEAT the LAMB
MEAT the STEAK
MEAT the BIRD

for any info. ask a member of staff :)

Butcher's Essay

Blimey! Where to start?

It's odd, but I have never really thought of myself as a butcher. I kind of 'fell' into the trade by accident. I had very little formal training and I have no qualifications. Well, I have now been at it for over 35 years, so I must know something, surely.

In Britain especially, it is the same for many butchers. As a nation, we have not been good at formal training for butchers and it has often been viewed as a trade for those suitable for nothing else. Historically, butchery has been a male-dominated profession. The long hours, heavy lifting and cold, dirty conditions were not considered conducive to young women. I wonder how many fathers dreamt of their cherished daughter becoming a butcher? Young boys would leave school, or even take up Saturday jobs, as soon as legally possible. They would be given the tedious, grubby, unsavoury tasks that the senior butchers didn't want to do. If they could stick it out, the boys would be moved onto some of the lesser jobs like mincing meat or making sausages, while also keeping the fridges scrubbed, the shop clean and running errands. Depending on the size of the shop, and the volume of business, sooner or later a young lad might get shown how to cut up a chicken, dice a chuck or de-bone a shoulder. Any training would be around the needs of the business. The needs of the employee would usually not get much consideration.

However, in more modern times, the pendulum has swung for the better. After the food scares of the 1990's and early 00's, the whole meat industry had to change, and small, independent butchery shops led the way. The public wanted more from their fresh food retailers. They wanted to know where the product came from and how it had been reared. Butcher's shops became cleaner, more boutique and more friendly to visit. The ambience changed. Using local shops and high streets became fashionable again and, as the butchery industry crept into the 21st century, it attracted a different type of mentality. In the last 20 years there has been a continuous and steady growth in the small, delightful, independent shop. In turn, this has changed what customers expect from their butcher.

Outside the cities, one still finds older, traditional butcher's shops. In villages and towns throughout Britain there are shops being manned by second and third generation traders, often family businesses. Speaking to these shopkeepers will quickly lead to stories of grandfathers, or great-grandfathers, being open all hours, serving the local community with ten times the amount of product sold today and, very often, stories of the animals being reared and slaughtered on the land. A quick rummage around any village bric-a-brac shop will lead to the discovery of an old black and white photo of the local butcher's shop with carcases hanging out front, framed by dozens of game birds in feather.

In the cities, however, it is a different landscape. There is more population, more disposable income and greater interest in modern food. New butcher shops are opening, some positively stylish. The customer wants more knowledge and a greater variety from their butcher. The customer comes to the shop now with a freshly Googled recipe or something from the glossy Sunday magazines. They ask for specific cuts, and often how to use them. As well as the traditional skills, contemporary butchers have had to acquire a new expertise in food and cooking.

Happily, the rise in consumer interest has seen a regeneration in our industry and the exciting new opportunity to bring on the next generation of butchers. Butchers in blood-splattered coats are a thing of the past and shops now invariably offer much more than just meat. The industry attracts young men and women looking to make a career in the food world.

Looking back at my time, I've been very lucky in my life to have worked with a great many international butchers. My butchery experience started in the early 1980s, during my apprenticeship with the Roux Restaurant group. I was lucky enough to be given a work placement at the beautiful Boucherie Lamartine in Paris, France. Even to my untrained eye, I knew that I was working with some of the finest tradesman that I would ever encounter. Their knowledge and deft skills were a wonder. Monsieur Prosper, the shop owner, came from generations of butchers and his son was just in the process of joining the business. His team varied in age, but each of them were exceptional. Not every shop in France would compete with Boucherie Lamartine, but the general standard of the French butcher has always been very high. the French took their butchery much more seriously than the British. It was considered a craft and the young people had formal training and gained formal qualifications. On returning from France, I helped open the Pimlico based butcher shop of the same name. It was designed specifically to supply the Roux Restaurant group with their meat, but it grew into many other things. We employed many

French boys and I came across a guy, Thierry Chenier, who became a very good friend, and was my assistant when I helped open Harvey Nichols' Foodmarket in 1992.

Later in life, from around 2006, I started to encounter Australian guys. They, too, came with portfolios of their training and state and National certification. In my experience, the Australians have been the best trained. They are always very capable and have a deep-seated knowledge of both method and product. Their customer service is always excellent, and they are always ready with a recipe and a story. The synergy of the barbecue and meat is obvious, and this, too, is where the Australians shine.

I have worked with butchers from many countries, each with their own traditions and cuts. I consider that I have seen the best and the not so good. As I write now, it's fantastic to consider that British butchers are now taking their place in the world order. Better training, more attention and greater interest have all aided the growth in skills and ability in the industry. A quick glance through a shop window on the high street, or a scroll across social media, will show a fantastic array of butchery skills that are now recognised in international competitions. It is striking how many chefs want to join the butchery industry and this, too, brings another great dynamic. Butchers are always going to be a funny old bunch, but it's an industry of skills, dedication and fun in equal measures. There are some amazing people and companies who share my views, dedicating themselves to training and the future. I would very much like to see a National Diploma of some description.

As many traditional, family businesses have declined, people have found other pathways to working as butchers. Modern technology, health and safety rules and Human Resource Law have all contributed in making the industry more user-friendly. A couple of year back, the winner of the Young Butcher of the Year – the top industry award – was a young woman. Bring it on!

My sawdust grumble...

So, what's all this nonsense about sawdust? It was all quite normal. The butcher would spread a couple of good handfuls of sawdust around the floors of his shop, and it would serve to soak up any dripping blood and keep the floor from getting too greasy. Like everything else, the best traders kept it looking clean, and would change it a couple of times a day (another job for the boy). Those that didn't care so much would leave it longer.

At some point around the late 80's, somebody, somewhere, decided that it was unhealthy. By the very nature of its name, it was dusty, and could be whipped up if the shop door was open for any period of time. It was considered unhealthy in case meat was dropped on the floor.

My point is that sawdust did a very good job and there has never been anything created to replace it. I take on board the health risks and, probably, thirty years later we would never go back to it. We don't have as much blood in shops these days as we used to, but it is very difficult to keep floors grease-free. I defy any butcher to cut down and prepare a lamb, for example, without getting any fat on the floor. The worst argument is the one relating to dropped meat. Anything that fell into sawdust was finished. The sawdust was never going to come off. Nowadays, there isn't an honest butcher alive who hasn't dropped a sausage and cited the 'three second rule' as he puts it back onto the display.

In truth, it's one of those subjects in life that really doesn't matter. I don't lie awake at night pining for sawdust, but not every change that is forced upon us happens for the better.

GRILLING
&
FRYING

Grilling & Frying

There is something deeply appetising about grilling or frying meat. The nostril-filling aromas that waft up when you cook this way are guaranteed to make you hungry. That wonderful smell of frying bacon really is irresistible. It's a very quick way of cooking. You need to be watching all the time and you need the right cuts of meat. Thin, portion-sized, tender cuts of meat work well here, such as escalopes, steaks, chops, chicken breast (skin on). Sausages, too, of course.

Which reminds me – when cooking poultry by 'direct' heat, that is grilling, frying, barbecue or in the oven, the skin protects the flesh from the heat and cooks nicely in its own right.

Something to bear in mind when grilling and frying is that the time taken carefully browning your meat really pays off. Not burning or blackening, which should be avoided, but achieving a nice brown hue on the meat. In 1912 a French chemist called Louis-Camille Maillard showed that browning food created a complex series of reactions that create flavour in the food – now named after him as the Maillard reaction. To put it in a nutshell, browning your meat makes it taste delicious!

Restaurants use an overhead grill called a salamander, which cooks the meat from above. Oven grills, too, work this way. A griddle pan cooks the meat from below. The benefit of getting the griddle pan smoking hot, and placing the meat gently across the bars, is that the bars sear the meat creating dark stripes that are full of intense flavour – yes, that Maillard reaction at work. One of the health benefits of grilling meat is that the fat melts and runs away, which is great for helping with a balanced diet. Mind you, let us not forget that animal fat is full of flavour. Barbecue cooking, of course, involves grilling and I explore that more fully in the barbecue section (p.88).

When it comes to pan-frying meat, a thick-bottomed frying pan – cast iron is best – does the trick. The thickness is important as it takes a higher heat, maintains the temperature and – if it's cast iron – can go from the stove to the oven, which is useful. The Spanish use a large, flat, solid iron surface called la plancha for cooking just about everything – the ultimate 'open' pan. When cooking beef steaks or chops, which need to be seared over a high heat, I spread seasoned oil over the meat first before placing it in the hot pan. Oiling the meat rather than the pan avoids burning the oil or creating too much smoke. For meat that requires gentler treatment – say a chicken breast or an escalope – I opt for shallow frying, heating the oil in the pan first, then carefully adding in the meat. Here the meat doesn't need such intense heat and benefits from being placed into a little warm oil. If you're frying a cut of meat that's a bit on the thick side and the outside is cooking too quickly while the inside is still raw, a useful tip is to cover the pan loosely with a lid. This concentrates the heat and speeds up the cooking. Don't use a tight-fitting lid though, as this creates steam and starts poaching.

For stir-frying – a fast, vigorous way of cooking – you need a wok as both its shape and size allows the small pieces of meat to cook quickly as they are moved around the pan with a spatula. Do remember to heat the wok through really thoroughly before you add in the oil and start stir-frying. You want that wok to be hot!

De-glazing

Once cooked, the meat will be removed from the pan, or griddle, and should be allowed to rest. At this point, it's a great trick to pour off any excess fats from the pan and then 'de-glaze' the pan. Keep the pan hot on the stove and add a liquid – usually stock, but wine, spirit or fruit juice would do. As the liquid comes to the boil, scrape the base of the pan vigorously with a spatula or wooden spoon to loosen all of the sediments and goodness resulting from the cooking. Remember when using spirit that there's a chance it will catch light, so be careful.

At this point, adding a knob of butter or a spoonful of double cream will give you a delicious sauce to accompany the rested meat. For a more refined sauce, pass the liquid through a fine sieve so as to remove any sediment.

Flavoured butters

Another quick way to add some flavour – and a little juice – to your chosen cut, is to use flavoured butters. There are some recipes on p.38 but really anything goes. Flavoured butters can be made well in advance and kept refrigerated or frozen. It is possible to melt a little of your flavoured butter in the pan and spoon it over your meat, but it is much nicer to cut a small disc from your flavoured butter roll, place it into the middle of the warm meat on the plate and let it melt on the way to the table.

23

GRILLING & FRYING:
STEAK

Thai Steak Salad

A steak salad with a difference! Thai flavours – salty, sweet, sour, hot – really lift this dish. The succulent steak strips contrast with the textures of the salad very nicely indeed. It's amazing how much flavour a simple marinade and a zingy salad dressing can deliver!

500g rump steak

¼ white cabbage, shredded

1 small courgette, grated

100g sugar snap peas, topped, tailed, chopped

8 cherry tomatoes, halved

3 tbsp salted peanuts, crushed

handful of mint leaves, torn

handful of coriander leaves, torn

2 tbsp crispy fried shallot (optional)

For the marinade:

1 lemon grass stalk

1 tsp whole peppercorns, roughly crushed

1 garlic clove, peeled and crushed

1 tbsp oil

1 tsp salt

For the dressing:

Juice of 1 lime

1 tsp sugar

2 tbsp fish sauce

1 tbsp sweet chilli sauce

First, make the marinade. Peel off the tough outer casing from the lemon grass stalk. Finely chop the lower, soft part of the stalk, discarding the fibrous remainder. Mix the lemon grass with the remaining marinade ingredients.

Finely slice the steak against the grain into short 0.5cm thick strips. Mix the steak strips with the marinade, coating evenly. Cover and chill for 1–2 hours.

Mix together the dressing ingredients. Taste the dressing – you're looking for a salty, sweet and sour flavour with a touch of chilli. Adjust to taste. Mix together the cabbage, courgette, sugar snap peas and cherry tomatoes. Just before you begin cooking the steak, toss the vegetables with the dressing and place in an even layer on a serving dish.

Pre-heat a barbecue or a griddle pan over a high heat on a stove top. Layer the steak strips in a single layer and cook for 1–2 minutes, then turn and cook for 1 minute on the other side.

Place the steak strips at once on the cabbage salad. Sprinkle over the crushed peanuts, mint and coriander leaves and crispy fried shallots, if using. Serve at once with jasmine rice or rice vermicelli.

Serves 4

Onglet Steak with Sauce Bordelaise

There are so many wonderful sauces that go well with steak. A full-of-flavour Sauce Bordelaise is right up there with the best of them. I couldn't imagine a medium rare onglet steak or a delicious bavette without the accompaniment of this marrow-enriched, shallot-flavoured, red wine-based favourite.

For the Sauce Bordelaise:

1 marrow bone, from which you want around 50g bone marrow

1 tbsp olive oil

1 tbsp finely chopped shallot

100ml red wine, preferably Bordeaux

1 sprig of thyme

100ml beef stock

Salt and freshly ground black pepper

4 onglet steaks, each around 200g, butterflied

1 tsp rapeseed or vegetable oil

Your butcher will be able to supply a marrow bone. Ask your helpful butcher for the marrow bone to be sawn into smallish pieces, around 2–3cm. To remove the marrow from the bone, warm a pot of water to a tepid temperature. Place the pieces of marrow bone in the water and set aside to warm up for a couple of minutes. Remove the bones from the water and, using your thumb, push the marrow from the bone onto a clean, cold plate and discard the bones.

To make the sauce, heat the olive oil in a frying pan. Add the shallot and, stirring constantly, fry until it takes on a golden-brown colour. Don't let the shallot burn as this will make it bitter.

Now, add the red wine and thyme to the pan. Bring to the boil, reduce the heat and simmer until reduced by about half.

Add the beef stock, stir in the marrow, bring to the boil and allow to reduce again until the sauce is thick enough to coat the back of a spoon. Season the sauce with freshly ground black pepper.

Meanwhile, heat your griddle or heavy bottomed pan until it starts to smoke. Rub your steak with the oil and season it with salt and black pepper. Lay the steak on the grill and allow it to cook for 1½ minutes, before turning it over and allowing to cook for 1½ minutes more. Remove the steak from the griddle and let it rest for 5 minutes in a warm place. This will give you a medium steak.

Put your steaks onto warm plates. Gently heat through the Borderlaise sauce and spoon a good helping onto each steak.

Beef, Mushroom and Red Pepper Stir-fry

I do love the drama of a stir-fry! Having everything already chopped and ready to go is the secret of a successful stir-fry. That and having the wok REALLY hot. The actual cooking is fast and furious, so be sure to have your accompanying rice or noodles ready.

350g rump steak

2 tbsp dark soy sauce

½ tsp salt

½ tsp freshly ground black pepper

2 dried Chinese mushrooms (dried shiitake), (optional)

2 tbsp oil

2 garlic cloves, chopped

2cm root ginger, finely chopped

2 spring onions, cut into 2cm lengths

½ red pepper, cut into short, fine strips

150g button mushrooms, cut into 1/2cm thick slices

1 tbsp rice wine or dry sherry

1 tbsp oyster sauce

Slice the steak across the grain into 1/2cm thick, 4–6cm long strips. Mix with 1 tbsp soy sauce, salt and pepper. Cover and set aside at room temperature to marinate for 30 minutes.

If using the Chinese mushrooms, which add a meaty flavour and texture to the dish, place them in a little bowl, pour over boiling water and soak for 25 minutes until softened. Drain and slice into strips, discarding the tough stalks.

Heat the wok over a high heat until very hot. Add in 1 tbsp oil, allow to heat through. Add in the beef strips and stir-fry briskly for 2 minutes, until they lose their raw pink look on all sides. Remove from the wok and reserve.

Wipe the wok clean. Heat through over high heat once again. Add the remaining oil and heat through. Add in garlic, ginger and white spring onion and stir-fry briefly until fragrant. Add in the red pepper and stir-fry for a minute. Add in the dried and fresh mushrooms and stir-fry to mix in. Return the beef strips to the wok.

Add in the rice wine and stir-fry for 1 minute, until it cooks off. Add the oyster sauce and remaining soy sauce, mixing well, and stir-fry for a further 1–2 minutes. Sprinkle over the green spring onion and serve at once with steamed rice or Chinese noodles.

Sauce Bearnaise

Some things are worth the time and this classic French sauce is right up there. Should I put the delicate, whipped sauce - fragrant with tarragon – on the steak or dip my chips into it?

300g unsalted butter

4 tbsp white wine vinegar

2 tsp chopped tarragon leaves

1 tsp finely chopped shallots

4 egg yolks

1 tsp lemon juice

2 tbsp tarragon leaves

First, clarify the butter. Melt it in a saucepan over a low heat. Once it begins to foam, remove from the heat and set it aside to cool, during which time white solids will form at the bottom of the pan. Gently and carefully, pour the liquid clarified butter into a container, discarding the solids.

Place the vinegar, chopped tarragon and shallots into a non-reactive saucepan. Bring to the boil and allow it to reduce by slightly more than a half. Strain the vinegar into a bowl and allow it to cool completely.

Place the egg yolks in a clean, dry bowl and add in 1tbsp cold water. Whisk together, then add in the reduced vinegar and the lemon juice, whisking in well.

Place the bowl with the egg yolk mixture over a pan of simmering water, making sure that the bottom of the bowl does not touch the hot water as that would cause the yolks to cook. Whisk the mixture vigorously until it thickens and doubles in volume.

Remove from the heat and slowly pour in the clarified butter, whisking constantly until the texture becomes soft and creamy. (If you want a romantic moment, get your partner to pour in the butter). Fold in the tarragon leaves and serve at once.

Sauce au Poivre – Peppercorn Sauce

Peppercorn sauce is a 'Marmite' sauce, not to everyone's taste. For me, its peppery punch combined with the luxurious creamy texture makes it a great accompaniment for many meat cuts. It is delicious with beef or pork steaks and just as delightful over chicken. If alcohol is not your thing, just don't add the brandy; the sauce will still taste as great.

3 tbsp peppercorns

60g unsalted butter

1 tbsp finely chopped shallot

1 tsp plain flour

50ml brandy

150ml beef stock

50ml double cream

Start by lightly crushing the peppercorns in a pestle and mortar. If you haven't got a pestle and mortar, you can crush the peppercorns with the end of a rolling pin. Crushing the peppercorns will create some 'dust'. Pour your crushed peppercorns into a fine sieve and shake gently to remove the dust. Set the crushed peppercorns to one side.

Melt the butter in a heavy-bottomed pan and sweat off the shallot over a low heat without letting it colour. Cook, stirring often, until the shallot becomes translucent. Add the flour and, stirring constantly to prevent it burning, cook the flour for a few moments.

Gently add the brandy and stir well into the flour, forming a paste. Gradually add in the beef stock while continuing to stir well. Be careful not to add the stock too quickly or lumps will form in the sauce. Once all the stock has been added and heated through and you're happy with the consistency of the sauce remove from the heat and stir in the peppercorns.

Put the pan back on the heat and whisk in the double cream and gently heat through. Cook to the consistency that you want and serve. Alternately, make the sauce in advance, cool and chill and reheat gently before serving.

Steaks

How evocative! Sitting around a table with friends. Maybe a bottle or two of an old world French Bordeaux or a stonking New World Malbec from Argentina, whiling away the time in anticipation of the arrival of a char-grilled beef steak, cooked just as you like it, crisp fluffy chips and the largest dollop of warm Bearnaise sauce.

It sounds a little old-fashioned, but actually it's timeless. People love their steak and chips just as much today as they always have and it's a classic on restaurant menus.

Steaks come in all shapes and sizes, but an average size of 200g to 250g will suit most appetites. In my opinion, a steak is a slice of meat that is cooked in the pan or on the grill. If the piece of meat needs to go in the oven to finish cooking, it's not really a steak any more. Your butcher should have had the beef hanging in the fridge for adequate time to allow the sinews to stretch and the muscles to relax and tenderise. How long beef should hang for is a matter of much conjecture, but the bigger steak joints – sirloin, forerib, rump or T-Bone – need at least 20 days. Fillet – a much softer cut – at least 10 days. Some butchers talk about aging beef for 40 days, or more, but my own view is that this is too long to hang meat on the bone. With modern technology, it is now possible to vacuum pack fresh meat with preserving gases and 'age' meat for much longer periods. This does tenderise the meat, but it – unlike traditional meat hanging – doesn't let the meat dry out and so intensify the flavour.

When buying a steak, look for a deep, rich red colour – much the same as your Bordeaux wine. The 'marbling' running through the middle of the meat should be white and clearly visible. The vein-y white lines are the fat and contain the magnificent flavours that we

The Method:

It takes approximately 8 minutes to cook an average size steak (200–250g about 2cm thick). For larger or smaller steaks, adjust the times accordingly.

Heat your griddle, or heavy bottomed pan, on the stove, until it smokes. It is important that it is really hot.

For a 'Rare' steak, cook for 1 minute on each side and then let it rest in a warm place for 6 minutes to ensure that the steak is not cold in the middle. For a 'medium' steak, cook for 2 minutes on each side and allow to rest for 4 minutes and for a 'well done' steak cook for 2 minutes on each side twice, so that each side has 4 minutes.

Chefs train for many years to perfect their skill. Don't beat yourself up if your steak isn't perfect first time. Just eat more steak and keep practising.

want. A strip of covering fat is another good marker. Three or four millimetres of cover is enough. Sometimes, if the meat has hung to its maximum, there may be a little mould under the skin. Some people like this mould but if it's not for you, ask your butcher to remove it.

A really good steak only needs to be lightly brushed with olive oil, seasoned with salt and pepper and put straight onto a searingly hot grill, or pan. As the outside chars the juices caramelise, creating savoury flavours. You need to turn your steak so that it continues to cook evenly from both sides. How long a steak takes to cook depends on a number of factors (the thickness, the temperature of the grill and the desired degree of 'cooking'). Learning to cook a steak to order is one of the key skills of the chef, but for those cooking at home see 'The Method' on the other page.

Fillet Steak

The softest and most tender of all beef cuts. Beef fillet is the most expensive of meat cuts. The fillet is a muscle that sits inside the animal, close to the vertebrae. It doesn't do anything and so never toughens up. It is practically fat-free, and so, if cooked too long, will dry out. The head of the fillet (Chateaubriande) sits inside the rump of the cow and the fillet stretches out along the loin, as it tapers to a thin tail at about 40/50cm. The centre cut of the fillet is deemed to be the best bit, but my own preference is a decent cut from the head. Possibly due to its the expense, a fillet portion is usually smaller than other steaks at about 170/200g. To my mind, best cooked in a pan and is okay on the grill. Not recommended for the barbecue.

Sirloin Steak

The sirloin runs along the back of the animal from the rump and takes on the first three rib bones. When prepared and matured properly, it is a tender cut without much fat running through it, though there should be a good covering of no more than 5mm on the top. An average sirloin steak weighs about 225–250g and be about a centimetre thick. It's a good choice for those preferring a 'well done' steak, but is a versatile cut. It's best on the grill and superb on the barbecue but quite happy in a pan. A very thin slice of sirloin – around 3–4mm – becomes a minute steak. The clue is in the name. It takes a minute to cook and is perfect for lunch but is not much use for those who want a rare steak.

Rib Eye Steak

Please remove your hat and pay attention. The King of Steaks has arrived! I will argue long and hard that the beef rib is as perfect a piece of meat as exists. As we come along the body, we start to see a line of gelatinous fat forming. In a well-bred, well prepared animal, the fat will be full of amazing flavour and will melt onto the plate when cooked. The beef rib is the four, or sometimes five, bones after the sirloin and benefits from the gelatinous fat running right through it. It is a versatile joint and I will return to it throughout the book, but as a boneless rib eye steak it has no equal. As the sirloin, about 225/250g and about one centimetre thick is a good portion. Now, I must point out that there are those people who are put off by fat on their plate. That's fine. Stay with the sirloin. The texture and flavour of the two steaks is similar. Seared on a hot grill, or in a hot pan, I choose my own steak 'medium'. It seems a shame to overcook a rib eye, but it will take 'well done' if necessary.

Rump Steak

The rump is at the top of the leg and is attached to the sirloin. It is one of three muscles that form the top part of the leg, but the only muscle which easily lends itself to steaks. By virtue of where it is, it's a hard-working muscle and needs a little more ageing than some of the others. We like to hang our rumps for up to 30 days to ensure that they are tender with a deep flavour. I use rump as a benchmark, if I am considering a new beef supplier or a different breed. Rump eats well but takes a bit more effort. It's for those who really love their steaks. 225–250g is sufficient and rump suits all of the usual cooking methods.

T-Bone Steak

This is the beast for a big eater, but the T-Bone also lends itself to sharing. If you think back to my description of the fillet, the sirloin and the rump, then the point where they all join is where we cut through the bone to achieve the T-Bone. The steak consists of a sirloin and a fillet, connected literally by a 'T' shaped bone. A small steak would weigh around 750g but at a reasonable thickness, 1kg would more like it. This is the steak that the Americans call the 'Porterhouse' and is really ideal for the grill. It's absolutely fantastic cooked on the barbecue over open coals.

Onglet (Thick Skirt or Hanger Steak)

I remember back to the 1980's, when I first started going to Smithfield Market, the cutters would literally throw the bag of onglet at us while muttering "dog meat" under their breath. It was so cheap to buy. Well, how times change. It was mostly sold in French restaurants, and French Chefs knew what to do with it. Other European countries also use it and in Britain it is often referred to as 'Skirt'. A bit like the fillet, the onglet comes from inside the animal, from the 'plate' or lower belly. It is very tender but bursting with flavour. It's still a little cheaper than other steaks, but now it costs more than 'dog food'! The onglet is delicious pan-fried, or grilled. It's so tender it doesn't need to be over cooked. Medium is ample.

Flat Iron (Butlers' Steak / Oyster Steak)

The flat iron has found its way onto restaurant menus and into butcher's shops in more recent times. It's a muscle from the shoulder of the cow. The muscle has an inedible, un-cookable sinew running through it which need to be removed. The steak takes its name from its resemblance to a flat iron. The meat is full of flavour and is best suited to the pan or grill. It is a good steak for marinating, but becomes quite tough if cooked past 'medium'.

Chuck Steak

Go straight to Beef (p.217) and I'll explain why we never grill chuck steak.

RIB-EYE S
Scottis

SIRLOIN STEAK
Scotch Beef

FILLET STEAK
Scotch Beef

Flavoured Butters

Making flavoured butters is so simple and they are a wonderful addition to a cook's repertoire. Pretty well any grilled or pan-fried piece of meat will work well with a flavoured butter. The only trick is to find the combination of meat and flavoured butter that you most enjoy.

Garlic & Parsley Butter

100g unsalted butter
1 tbsp finely chopped curly parsley
1 garlic clove, crushed
1 twist of freshly ground black pepper

Anchovy Butter

100g unsalted butter
3 anchovy fillets, finely chopped
1 twist of freshly ground black pepper

Sage and Lemon Butter

100g unsalted butter
½ tbsp finely chopped sage leaves, mixed with 1 tsp lemon juice to prevent discolouring
1 twist of freshly ground black pepper

Chive Butter

100g unsalted butter
1 tbsp finely chopped chives
1 twist of freshly ground black pepper

Wild Garlic Butter

100g unsalted butter
1 tbsp chopped wild garlic
1 twist of freshly g round black pepper

Smoked Paprika Butter

100g unsalted butter
1 tbsp smoked paprika
1 tsp runny honey

The Method

Let the butter soften to room temperature. Put it into a clean bowl, add the other ingredients (see suggestions above) and mix them all together. I find using a rubber spatula makes the task very easy and you can then scrape the butter out of the bowl when it's ready.

When the butter is well mixed, flatten a sheet of cling film (about 20 cm) onto a clean work surface and place the flavoured butter in the middle. Fold the cling film over the butter and start to roll it into a cylindrical shape. Keep rolling until the butter is about 4cm in diameter. When the cylinder is formed, roll it firmly in the cling film, twist the ends of the cling film tightly and refrigerate the butter until you want to use it. The butter will last 3–4 days in the fridge. It can be frozen if you want to get ahead.

When you are ready to use your butter, lay the cylinder on your cutting board and, with a sharp, warm knife cut a disc about 1cm thick for each piece of meat. If your butter has been frozen, you will need to let it soften a little before trying to cut it. Remember to remove the cling film outer before serving on top of the hot meat. The butter will continue to melt as you serve the dish to the table. Another option is to melt the butter in a pan and pour it over the meat.

Full English Breakfast

The meal of champions. There is something very special about a 'full English breakfast'. On busy weekdays I am happy to start my day with Greek yoghurt and honey, while Mrs Grout enjoys muesli with fresh berries. When it comes to the weekend, however, and you're looking for a meal to set you up for the day, then really nothing beats a proper cooked breakfast.

So, here's what I would want to see for my full English…

1 large Cumberland sausage or 2 chipolatas – grilled
1 rasher smoked middle-cut bacon – grilled
1 fried egg (maybe 2) – fried
1 slice of black pudding – fried
2 diced field mushrooms – fried
1 slice of wholemeal toast
Grapefruit juice
Coffee with warm milk (no sugar, please)

Cumberland Sausage

It disappoints me that the average B&B, hotel or café pays so little attention to sausages at breakfast. In a country that boasts so many great sausage makers, it's just penny-pinching and lazy. I've chosen a Cumberland sausage because they are full of flavour while remaining a little neutral. I don't want the leek flavour of a Welsh Dragon sausage or the paprika from a Chorizo. A really good, garlicy Toulouse is delicious for lunch or dinner but not for breakfast. The Cumberland is a pork sausage with a little thyme, sage, coriander, parsley and mace. One good size sausage should be enough, while for those who prefer a chipolata, then go for two.

Smoked Middle-Cut Bacon

Bacon is about individual taste, but the smell of smoked bacon first thing in the morning is a wonderful thing. The key to good bacon is, obviously, good pork. The streaky is made from the belly and has those natural fats running through it. I like back bacon, from the loin, and for those who aren't keen on smoked foods, the unsmoked is fine. However, for that special breakfast, I like the combination of the back and the streaky, the middle-cut (sometimes known as the 'through' cut). It's bordering on the old fashioned these days, and not everyone sells it. It's pretty much the whole side of the pork and brings together all of the textures and flavours. One rasher is going to be a large piece, and a decent portion for breakfast.

Fried Egg

A soft-boiled egg is great in an egg cup with toasted soldiers, and no, you're never too old for a dippy egg. Scrambled egg is delicious on toast and even better if garnished with a little smoked salmon, or a sprinkling of chopped chives, and, for breakfast, poached eggs are at their best buried under a thick blanket of soft, creamy Hollandaise sauce. A good, fresh, free-range fried egg is the only way to go. Lightly cooked and 'sunny side' up (the egg is not flipped and the yolk is visible and runny). Seasoned with a light sprinkling of good salt and a twist of black pepper, the yolk is the condiment for your breakfast. Put it into the middle of the plate and let it be the star of the show.

Black Pudding

I love the boudin noir from France and every Spanish region creates a morcilla to die for, but we British still make the best blood sausage. The European sausages are softer and more puréed. Our British pudding is coarser, and the best one's have a few small lumps of fat visible throughout. At Meat London we usually get our black pudding from Grants of Speyside in Aberdeen, simply because it's so good. The average pudding is around 6cm in diameter, and a 2cm thick slice will be a good portion. I know black pudding isn't everyone's choice, but my breakfast needs it.

Mushrooms

It's strange how tastes change. As a kid, I couldn't stand mushrooms, but when I started my apprenticeship, I wasn't given the choice as to whether I wanted to eat them or not. One of my first jobs was cooking omelettes, and I had to taste the mushrooms I cooked and put inside. Over time, I came to really enjoy them and now they certainly make my perfect breakfast plate. There are many different types, but, for me, wild mushrooms are not suitable for a Full English – too delicate and also a bit too grand for breakfast. Button mushrooms will do, but I think that field mushrooms are just the job. Cut off the stalk and peel off the outer skin. It's worth the effort.

Toast

Buttered toast! Two words that it's worth getting out of bed for. I don't want it 'under' anything, and I want it warm. Straight from under the grill, or out of the toaster, buttered and brought to the table. One slice is enough. I've chosen wholemeal bread as it's invariably delicious and is probably that little bit more healthy (a strange consideration at the end of my breakfast list, I know!). My other choice would be a slice of good, home-made crusty white bread, untoasted and buttered. I had to think about this one, but I'm just leaning towards the toast.

What's missing?

Baked beans, from those people with 56 other varieties, should be a consideration, but I prefer mushrooms and I don't think there's space for both. Hash browns or chips are not for me. I don't need potatoes for breakfast. Anyway, hash browns are an American thing and have no place in a classic Full English. However, I do admit that tossing last night's left-over spuds in a little olive oil and butter is delicious.

Now, breakfast chefs of the world, please take note. Luke-warm, half grilled tomatoes are horrible. The tomato is such a wonderful, versatile vegetable – it deserves better. I'm not adverse to cooked plum tomatoes, but they don't make my best breakfast list. When it comes to condiments, I can never make up my mind what I want in advance, so we always put brown and red sauce on the table.

What to drink

Freshly squeezed fruit juice is a must. My own preference is a really good grapefruit, but I'm partial to orange as well. I've tried apple juice but it's not great for breakfast (better with vodka in the evening). I don't like smoothies, or anything blended actually and, again, they are too heavy as part of a Full English. Now here's a thing? Should coffee be part of a Full English, or should it be all about a mug of tea? Well, I think we have probably been drinking coffee for long enough in Britain to accept it. Anyway, I couldn't start my day without a decent cup of coffee. I don't know why we can't replicate French breakfast coffee. I think it's probably the milk, but it is the best and it does matter if the milk is warm or not. Cold milk makes the coffee go cold too quickly. I've only put 'no sugar' in the ingredients in case a customer wants to bring me a cup one morning.

And there you are. My favourite breakfast. It's not really mind-blowing, or anything out of the ordinary, but using good ingredients, and cooking them properly makes all the difference to the best meal of the day.

Chops

I was born in Clapham, South London, to a typically working class family. There weren't many airs and graces, but, as children, we were taught how to behave and how to do things properly. Every second Sunday mum and dad took my two sisters and I on the Northern Line to Morden, where Pop (my Grandad) picked us up and took us to Sunday lunch, cooked by my nan. My aunts and uncles would be there, and my only cousin on my father's side. It was a real family occasion. Pop sat at the head of the table and nanny just kept bringing more and more food. Everybody sat up straight, no elbows on the table, no talking with full mouths and no leaving without asking to be excused. Us children were asked questions, and we were expected to answer properly. But here's a funny thing; if we couldn't get to the food with our knife and fork, we were encouraged to use our fingers. To this day, in my opinion, there are a few things that never taste the same when speared with a fork. Asparagus, chips and a really good chop are at the top of my list.

Chops come in all shapes and sizes, and from every animal. A chop is defined as the cut of meat still on the bone. Chops mostly come from the saddle (loin) or the rib cage (best end/rack). A typical chop should be about an inch thick with a juicy, round eye and a good, even covering of fat. Including the bone, a 300g chop should be an adequate portion, but allow up to 400g for a special treat. 'Cutlet', by the way, is just another name for a chop. There's no real reason why some chops get the moniker 'cutlet'.

Chops are a tasty and versatile cut. Think of a man-size pork chop with nicely crackled skin, dainty lamb chops bursting with flavour, a classic veal cutlet to a beef forerib. A plain cooked chop is delicious enough, but chops lend themselves to being seasoned with herbs or spices, marinaded and served with sauces.

When asking your butcher to cut you a chop, you need to consider what and how you want to cook it. A simply grilled pork chop, served with green vegetables or a side salad, makes a great simple meal. For a dinner party, lamb chops or a delicate veal cutlet seem more suitable. Generally speaking, chops are little thicker than many cuts and after creating flavour by browning in a pan, or on the grill, may well need to be finished in a preheated oven. Not too long in the oven. Cooking times depend on the size of the chop and how 'done' you want the meat, but rarely more than 10 minutes.

Caution: A chop should be a mixture of lean meat and some of its fatty surrounds. 'French' trimming the top of the bone is acceptable only because the practice removes the mostly fatty top section, exposing a bit of bone with which to hold the chop. The habit of over-enthusiastic chefs of trimming the poor chop back so far that it is no more than a tiny piece of meat flapping around at the bottom of the bone should be considered a crime against the chop.

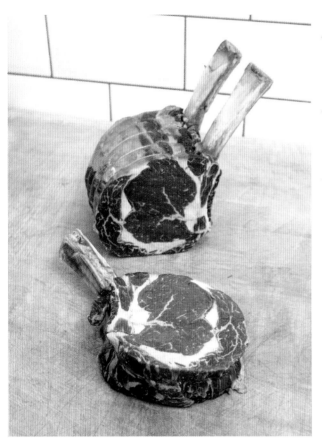
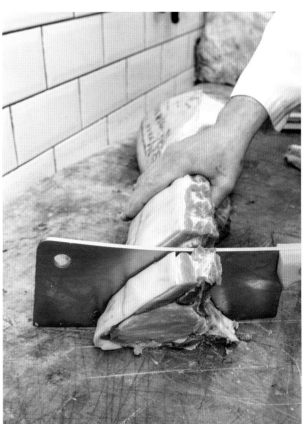

Serves 4

Veal Cutlets with Sage and Lemon Butter

Veal divides opinion. Some people detest it for what it is. Some people don't like the mild, soft flavour, while others love it. This recipe is simplicity itself, but makes for a delicious meal.

2 tbsp vegetable oil

Salt and freshly ground pepper

4 veal cutlets, each 250–300g

4 knobs sage and lemon butter (see p.39)

1 lemon, cut into four wedges

Put the oil in a large, flat dish. Season the oil liberally with salt and cracked black pepper. Add the cutlets to the dish and coat them well in the seasoned oil.

Heat a griddle pan until it just starts to smoke. Drain the oil from the cutlets and lay them at an angle across the bars of the griddle. Always place the meat into the pan away from you to avoid splashing.

After one minute, turn the cutlets from the bottom, so that again you place it away from you. After another minute, turn the cutlets again, but this time the other way across the griddle, away from you.

Finally, after one more minute turn the cutlets for the final time. After the last minute, four in total, remove the cutlets from the griddle, into a warm dish and let it rest for four minutes. If you have turned the cutlets the right way, you will have beautiful criss-crosses seared into the meat. Let the meat rest in a warm place for four more minutes.

Serve the warm cutlets onto four warm plates and put a knob of sage and lemon butter on top of each one. Place a lemon wedge on the side of each plate.. Take the plates to the table as the butter melts.

Barnsley Chops with Garden Herbs

I may be repeating myself. Generally speaking, prime English lamb needs very little else. A few garden herbs, though, will enhance the flavour. The other one of my rules broken here, is that of 'grilling' happening on top of the stove. A good Barnsley chop will be 2cm thick. Those wanting their lamb a little more than medium cooked (me!) will need to give the chops a few minutes in the oven to avoid burning the outside.

A Barnsley Chop is a cut across the whole lamb saddle, offering two chops for one serving. However, it is sometime easier, and more manageable to cut the chop in half, technically creating two loin chops, but let's not be pedantic (unless you come from Barnsley, in which case, I apologise for my frivolity).

½ tsp finely chopped thyme

½ tsp finely chopped rosemary

½ tsp finely chopped oregano

¼ tsp finely chopped sage

1 garlic clove, crushed

1–2 tbsp rapeseed or vegetable oil

4 Barnsley chops (or 8 loin chops)

Mix the herbs, garlic and oil in a large bowl. If the mixture looks a bit dry, add another tablespoon of oil and mix well again.

Add the chops to the bowl and rub well with the herb mix. Place the chops into a flat dish, cover with clingfilm and rest at room temperature for about 30 minutes.

Heat a dry grill pan, or a heavy based frying pan, until the first signs of smoke. Carefully lay the chops onto the grill and allow to cook for 1 minute. Turn the chops onto their other side and cook for 1 minute. Now turn the chop back onto the first side and cook for a third minute. Finally, turn again and cook for a fourth minute on the second side.

Remove the chops from the pan, back into the marinating dish, and allow to rest in a warm place for four minutes. This will provide medium to medium-rare chops. If you want them a little more cooked – medium to well done – put them into a pre-heated oven (200°C) for four minutes before resting.

Serve to the table on warm plates with something delicious – ratatouille in the winter, a green salad in the summer, or gratin Dauphinoise anytime.

Pork Chump Milanese

Serves 4

Shallow-frying breadcrumbed meat always makes a meal into a treat. Here I'm using the pork chump – an old-fashioned cut that sits between the leg and the loin and is full of flavour. Making this is a job to get the kids involved in. How much mess can you possibly make with a pork steak, flour, egg and breadcrumbs?

6 tbsp plain flour

4 eggs, beaten

6–8 tbsp panko breadcrumbs

4 pork chump steaks, skin removed,
 ask the butcher to beat them flat
 and even to about ½ cm thickness

Salt and pepper

Vegetable oil, enough to cover your frying pan to 2–3mm

30g butter, per batch

4 lemon wedges

Sieve the flour onto a clean dry plate. Tip the beaten eggs into a dish big enough to take the steaks. Finally, pour the panko breadcrumbs onto another plate.

Lay the steaks on your board and season them with salt and pepper. Put each steak into the flour and coat on both sides. Lift the steak out of the flour and shake off any excess. Too much flour will make a lumpy mess in your pan. Now do the same thing with the egg mixture, remembering to shake off any excess, and lastly, into the breadcrumbs. Push the steak down into the breadcrumbs to make sure they stick well. Repeat the process with each steak, one at a time.

When the chump steaks are ready, heat enough oil gently in your heavy bottomed pan and add 30g butter. As the butter starts to foam, place the meat into the pan, always remembering to place the meat away from you, so as to avoid splashes with hot fat. Control the heat and don't let the oil get too hot. Depending on the size of your pan, you may need to cook the meat in batches. After two minutes, turn the steak. The first side should be golden brown. Cook for another two minutes, basting the meat with the oil and butter during cooking. Remove the meat from the pan and keep it to one side, in a warm place, for a further two minutes.

Serve each chump steak on a warm plate with a wedge of lemon. You could serve a small bowl of Salsa Verde on the side (p.78).

Gammon & Bacon

Who can resist the tempting aroma of bacon cooking? Just thinking about it makes me want to fast forward to Sunday breakfast. It's almost worth getting a hangover simply to justify the restorative powers of a couple of thick rashers of bacon between two slices of bloomer with lashings of tomato ketchup!

While people know what bacon is, gammon is less familiar. In fact, they're both prepared in pretty much the same way by curing pork, either by dry-curing or wet-curing. Both can be smoked or un-smoked (known as 'green') but always need to be cooked at the end of the curing process.

Gammon is specifically the hind leg of the pig. Once cured, whether cooking the gammon on the bone or off the bone, it is often poached in water, stock or cider. The cooking process is where gammon changes to ham. Thickly sliced, boneless gammon produces the most delicious steak to be grilled or fried.

Bacon, on the other hand, mainly comes from the middle of the pig: the loin or belly, or both. The belly produces 'streaky' bacon, the loin produces 'back' bacon and if both cuts are kept as one, this is known as 'middle-Cut' or 'through-Cut' bacon. Collar bacon, from the neck area, is another cut, but one which is rarely seen nowadays.

How the bacon is cured affects the final texture and flavour. With wet brining, the liquid gets absorbed by the meat. Unscrupulous producers may even pump or inject brine into the muscle to increase the weight. The result is often a pan or grill full of unpleasant liquid leaked from the bacon as it cooks. Dry curing increases the intensity of flavour, similar to the aging process of beef. The meat to be cured will be rubbed with salts, herbs and natural preservatives and, nowadays, vacuum packed for ten to fifteen days, depending on the density and size of the cut. After this curing, un-smoked bacon is unwrapped and left to rest for at least 24 hours in order to dry out before slicing and cooking. For smoked bacon, the cured meat is hung in a smoking chamber and cold smoked for around eight hours, a process which imparts a smoky flavour to the food without cooking it.

Pancetta and guanciale are also part of the bacon 'family'. Pancetta is cured belly, usually smoked, and brings a smoky savouriness to stews, sauces and pasta dishes. Guanciale is cured pig's cheek, typically used in spaghetti alla carbonara or bucatini all'amatriciana, once again bringing a deep flavoursome richness.

Gammon with Mustard Sauce

Serves 4

Gammon is cured pork from the back leg and makes a delicious alternative to bacon. I'm never sure if I want gammon for breakfast, lunch or a quick supper. The mustard sauce in this recipe does make this more of a lunch or supper dish.

4 smoked or unsmoked gammon steaks, each about 150g
1 tbsp vegetable oil
2 tbsp Dijon mustard
75ml vermouth
125ml chicken stock
2 tbsp crème fraiche
1 tsp chopped curly parsley

Heat a heavy bottomed frying pan on the stove. Rub the gammon steaks with oil. Gammon is naturally salty, so I choose not to season them further. Carefully lay the steaks into the pan and fry for 2 minutes before turning and frying for another 2 minutes. Remove the steak to a holding dish and keep them warm. Depending on the size of your pan, you may need to cook the gammon in batches.

Pour off any excess fats but keep the natural juices in the pan. Add the mustard and stir well. Then add the vermouth and mix well with the mustard. The vermouth is likely to catch light, so be ready. Allow the alcohol to burn off. Reduce the liquid by half and then add the stock. Bring to the boil and sieve into a clean pan. Allow the sauce to reduce by half once more or until thick enough to coat the back of a spoon.

Whisk in the crème fraiche, bring to the boil and add the parsley.

Serve the gammon steaks on warm plates with the sauce. A good portion of hot crispy chip is an excellent side. Towards the end of the asparagus season, when the asparagus gets a little thicker, I would happily serve steamed asparagus with this dish.

GRILLING & FRYING:
POULTRY & GAME

Grilled Pheasant Breast with Wild Mushroom Sauce

Serves 4

Wild mushrooms are seasonal, with autumn to spring the best time of year to find them. If you can't find fresh wild mushrooms, use a mixture of fresh mushrooms – field, chestnut, shiitake, king oyster – together with flavourful dried porcini (cep) and morels. Make sure that the dried mushrooms have been well soaked in warm water to rehydrate them properly before you start cooking. Pairing your wild mushroom sauce with pheasant brings all of the flavours of the country into your kitchen and conjures up ideas of a long walk with friends and family before lunch.

4 pheasant supremes, skin on

1 tbsp olive oil

Salt and freshly ground pepper

For the wild mushroom sauce:

1 tbsp olive oil

30g butter

2 tsp chopped shallot

300g wild mushrooms, wiped clean, hard ends trimmed, sliced not too thinly

70ml vermouth

150ml white stock (see p.265)

100ml double cream

1 tbsp chopped curly parsley

Salt and freshly ground pepper

Heat your griddle or heavy bottomed frying pan on the stove.

Rub the pheasant with 1 tbsp olive oil and season with salt and pepper. Keep to one side in a dish.

For the sauce, heat the olive oil and butter in a separate heavy bottomed pan and fry off the shallots for a minute. Add the mushrooms and continue to fry gently until they are cooked through. Don't let the mushrooms overcook. Season well with salt and pepper. Carefully remove the mushrooms from the pan with a slotted spoon and keep on one side. Leave the juices in the pan.

Return the pan to the heat, pour in the vermouth and let the pan deglaze. The vermouth may well catch light. Allow the alcohol to burn off, but keep a lid handy to put out the flames. Add the stock and bring to the boil. Allow the liquid to reduce by half and then add the cream. Stir well and bring to the boil. Cook the sauce until it thickens to your preferred consistency. Turn off the heat.

Lay the pheasant breasts skin side down into the preheated griddle or pan. Allow to cook for 1 minute before turning over and cooking for another minute. Adjust the heat of your pan to ensure that the pheasant doesn't burn. Turn back onto the skin side for 1 more minute, and finally, turn one last time for another minute. Remove the pheasant from the pan and keep warm.

Add the mushrooms back into the sauce and bring to the boil, stirring well. Finish with the chopped parsley and season to taste.

Lay the pheasant out on warmed serving dish, and spoon the delicious wild mushroom sauce on top.

Chicken Schnitzel

I'm pretty sure that the schnitzel originated in Austria (Wikipedia agrees!) and usually refers to gently beaten cuts of meat or poultry that have been breadcrumbed. This chicken version takes me back to winter ski slopes. Age and dodgy knees have beaten me now and I probably won't ski again, but that won't dim my memories of the exhilaration of so many ski holidays.

4 chicken fillets

6 tbsp plain flour

salt and freshly ground pepper

4 eggs, beaten

10 tbsp panko breadcrumbs

2 tbsp vegetable oil

50g butter

a little finely chopped parsley, to garnish

If you haven't got the time or inclination, ask your butcher to beat the chicken fillets to just less than 1cm thick. If you want to do it yourself, it's very therapeutic to get two pieces of greaseproof paper or clingfilm, put a chicken fillet between them and whack it firmly with your rolling pin. A caution, however – if you want the chicken to cook evenly, you need to beat it out evenly.

Spread the flour on a plate and season it with salt and pepper. Place the beaten eggs in a large shallow bowl and the breadcrumbs on another plate. Start by coating the first chicken fillet in the flour. Lift it out of the flour and shake off all the excess. Too much flour at this stage will make a lumpy mess in your pan. Now dip the fillet into the egg and, again, lift it out and shake off the excess. Finally, into the bread crumbs and press down gently on both sides of the chicken, to ensure that the crumbs stick. Set aside and repeat the process with the remaining fillets. Now, the process is that the flour sticks to the chicken, the eggs stick to the flour and the crumbs stick to the egg. If you're tempted to cut corners and do all four at once, you are going to get into a mess. There, I've warned you.

Heat the oil in a heavy-based, large frying pan over a medium heat. Add the butter and let it melt until it starts to foam. Carefully lay your chicken fillets into the pan. Always lay the meat away from you so as not to splash yourself with hot oil. If your pan is big enough, you can fry all of the chicken together, but if not, cook it in two batches. Let the chicken cook in the oil and butter for two minutes and then turn it over, for a further two minutes. The bread crumbs should become golden brown, without burning. Control the cooking by turning the heat down if you need to. Once both sides are golden, remove the chicken from the pan and keep in a warm place to rest for a few minutes.

Put all four chicken fillets onto a warm serving dish, season with a little salt and pepper and sprinkle the chopped parsley on top. Serve to the table with your best smile.

Serves 4

Venison Haunch Steak with Cumberland Sauce

When it comes to game, I get all moralistic. All game should be hunted and we should only take what we are going to eat. To this end, all of the venison we sell is wild. There are some very good farmed animals available, but it's not for me. Game with Cumberland Sauce is very British and I sit up a little straighter when I eat it.

2 tbsp vegetable oil

Roughly ground black pepper and salt

4 venison haunch steaks, each about 200g

For the Cumberland sauce:

1 orange

1 lemon

300g redcurrant jelly

125 ml port

½ tsp English mustard

½ tsp ground ginger

Pour the vegetable oil into a shallow dish and season the oil with pepper and salt. Heat up a griddle pan, looking for the first smoke.

Put the venison steaks into the seasoned oil and ensure that they well coated. Remove the steaks from the dish, allowing any excess oil to run back into the dish. Carefully place the steaks onto the griddle and cook for one minute. Turn onto the other side and grill for another minute. Do this twice more before removing the steaks from the heat and letting them rest in a warm place for four minutes.

Peel the zest from the orange and lemon. Slice as finely as possible. Place the zest in a bowl and pour boiling water on top. Allow the zest to soften in the water for 4–5 minutes, which will also remove any bitterness. Juice the orange and lemon.

Place the redcurrant jelly and port in a heavy bottomed saucepan. Gently bring to the boil, stirring regularly, until the jelly has melted.

Meanwhile, in a clean bowl, mix the mustard and the ginger with the orange and lemon juice. Whisk well, then add in port and redcurrant jelly mixture, and whisk again. Pour into a sauce boat and stir in the softened orange and lemon zest.

Place each of the venison haunch steaks onto a warm plate and top with one turn of black pepper. Serve accompanied with the delicious Cumberland Sauce.

GRILLING AND FRYING:
SAUSAGES AND BURGERS

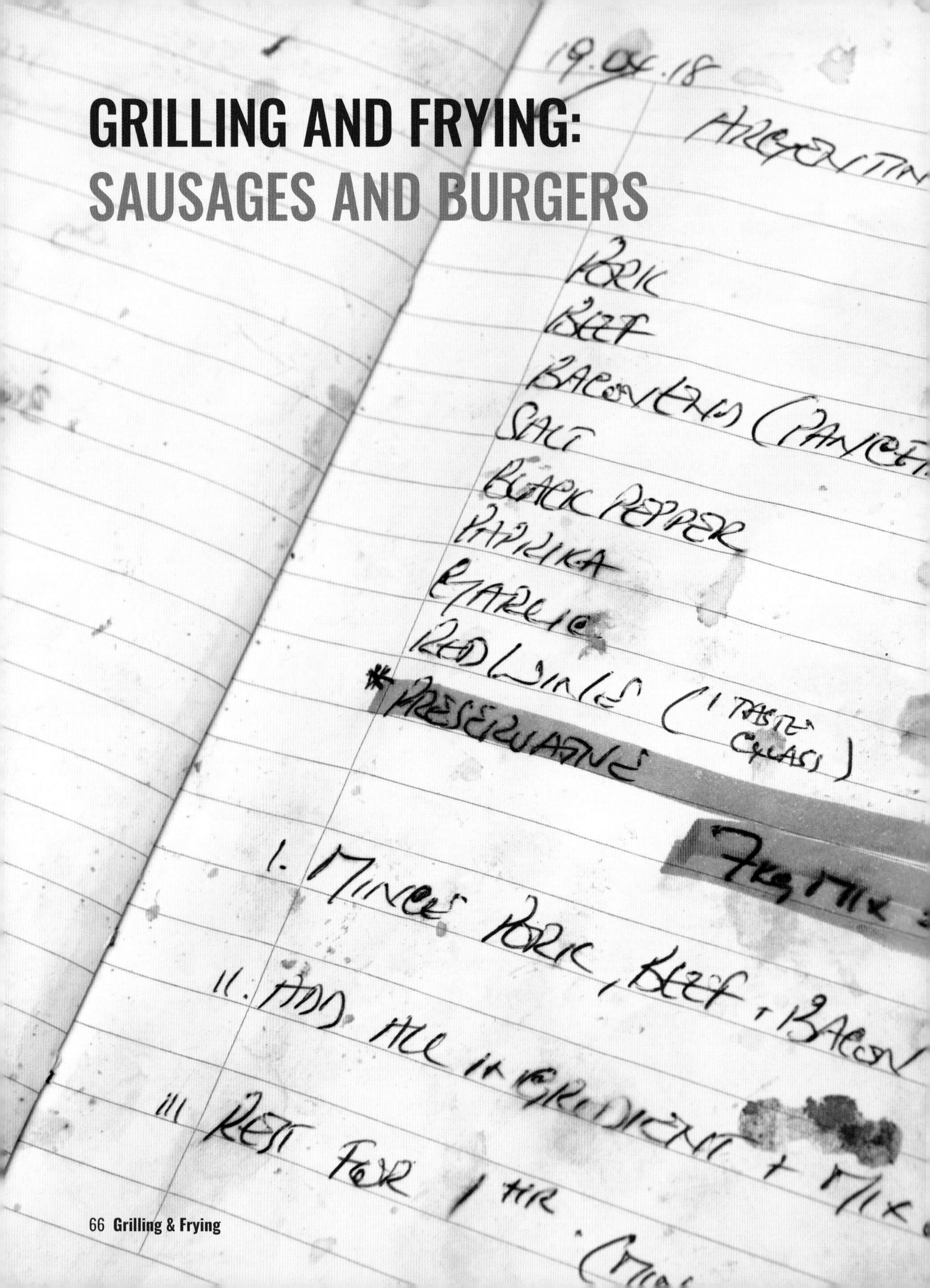

19.04.18

ARGENTIN

PORK

BEEF

BACON ENDS (PANCETT

SALT

BLACK PEPPER

PAPRIKA

GARLIC

RED WINE ("TASTE" GLASS)

* PRESERVATIVE

FRY MIX

1. MINCE PORK, BEEF + BACON

II. ADD ALL INGREDIENT + MIX

III REST FOR 1 HR . (THE

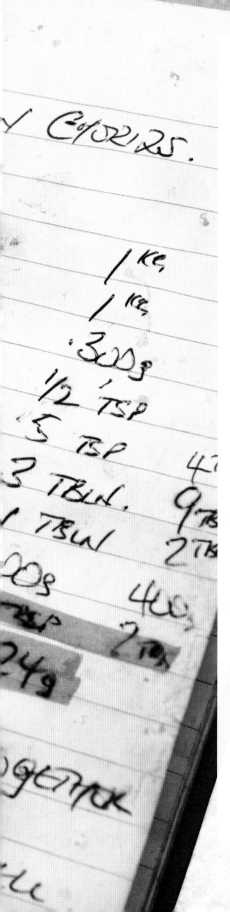

Sausages

The very thought of a sausage stirs up emotions and enthusiasm. How can something so simple and accessible be so loved throughout the land, and be the subject of so much debate and opinion? From the breakfast tables of Britain's great houses to the finest restaurants and hotels and the much-loved local café, sausages have been a staple part of British cuisine for as long as anyone can remember.

Of course, the refrigerator is a relatively recent invention. The early pioneers of sausage making would have been producing cured sausages, similar to what we now know as salami, saucisson or salchichon. The word sausage itself derives from the Latin salsus, meaning 'something salted'. Salt, of course, essential for curing meat. There is reference to sausages in Greek literature as far back as 2000 years ago, and it is known that the Romans were great sausage makers. During the winter months in northern Europe, it was possible to make and keep fresh sausages.

Sausages are a fine example of nose to tail eating. In the case of pork sausages, the pig's small intestine has historically been used for a natural casing and filled with finely chopped meat. In British butchery, pork, beef and lamb are the main meats that we use. It is honest to recognise that, in the not too distant past, sausages were very much the 'dumping' ground of the butcher's shop. Anything that was looking a little tired, or on its last legs, was very likely to find its way into the mincer to be transformed into sausages. But the tide has turned. Today any butcher worthy of the name will be using top quality meat to make the finest sausages. At Meat London, meat from the same pork carcase that we cut pork chops or a classic Sunday roast goes into our sausages. The same goes for our beef, lamb and chicken sausages. We prepare our animals and take away the 'prime' cuts, leaving what might be considered as secondary cuts to use for mince, stews, braising and, of course, sausages. More so than possibly any other product, the correlation of what we put in, and the quality of what we get back, is evident in the Great British Banger. By the way; it is thought that the 'banger' name came about because sausages made with too much fatty meat or too much water, then cooked over a hot, open fire, would 'explode', bursting their skins. Although sausage production is much improved today, the 'banger' nickname stays with us.

As well as using the best meat, what other ingredients do you need for a good sausage? The first thing to understand is that sausages need fat; this helps explain why the quality of the animals that we use is so important. As a rule of thumb, about 20% of the meat content of our sausages will be fat. If there was no fat in a sausage, then it would dry out in the cooking process and we would be left with a dry, unpalatable mix in our mouths.

One issue is how much meat should there be in a sausage? Anyone claiming 100% meat in their sausages hasn't accounted for seasoning, flavourings, bread or rusk or arguably even the skin. People proclaim the virtues of sausages made without any bread or rusk at all. But bread binds the ingredients and adds to the shelf-life of the sausage. Used in the right proportions, bread or rusk adds to the quality of the sausage, but if used as a 'filler', to replace or reduce the meat content, then it detracts. Water makes the sausage meat easier to use and helps to get the meat into the skin evenly and so helps with the linking process. Generally, if one allows 75%–80% meat, 10% bread or rusk, 10% water plus seasoning and flavourings, you are not going to be far away from a decent sausage. The art of linking sausages, by the way, is a very British thing. This process uses the casing itself to seal each sausage. In other countries sausages are usually tied with string. Linking sausages is one of the skills our team learn early on.

To complete our sausages, we need to get them into their skins (casings). It would be easy to write that one should only use natural casings. For dietary, religious and health reasons, however, there is a place for synthetic, collagen-based sausage skins. My ideal sausages, however, are made using natural skins. In principle, the sausage skin is from the animal intestine. Lamb for chipolatas or cocktail sausages, pig for typical British sausages and cow, or maybe horse, for larger sausages or cured, salami style. Sausage skins are pretty robust and, when filled properly, they are easy enough to use

The final step a good butcher takes that adds to the quality of their sausages, is to 'rest' or 'hang' freshly-made sausages for between 24 and 48 hours before selling them. During this time, the meat settles and contracts, the skins will dry out and much of the water drains away.

At Meat London, we enjoy creating sausage recipes. Making sausages can be done at home as well. You can buy table top mincers and stuffers and most kitchen aides come with sausage-making attachments. Unlike baking or patisserie, sausage making is not an exact science. It lends itself to creative experimentation. Select your preferred meat, get your bread and water ready and use your imagination to come up with delicious flavours. A walk along the river might see you foraging wild garlic, a stroll around the garden might offer garden herbs or fruit and – my favourite – a rootle around the back of the cupboard might unearth that gift set of dried herbs and spices that your Aunt bought you for Christmas last year. Have fun! Mix it all together, but before filling your casings, make a little patty, fry it up and taste your handiwork. This gives you the chance to adjust the flavouring and seasoning.

There are two questions that we get asked in our shops every day. Where can I buy sausage skins? Should I prick my sausages before cooking"? The answer to the first is that any butcher making sausages in their own shop, has sausage skins for sale. If your butcher does not have skins for sale, it's very likely that they are not making their own sausages. And to prick or not to prick? I have been in catering since I left school at 16 years of age. I have worked with some of the finest farmers, producers and chefs that have graced our shores and there is no general agreement. Me? I don't prick my sausages.

WILD BOAR &
APPLE SAUSAGE

wild boar with apples

Cont

TOULOUSE
SAUSAGES

Pork, Garlic, Herbs,

WELSH DRAGON
SAUSAGES

Free Range Pork, Leeks, Chilli, Seasoning

Cont

Sausages with Lentils

Serves 4

I like the earthiness of pulses. They always make me think of cold nights and sharing food with friends. Lentils top my list. They are already full of flavour, but embrace everything thrown at them as their friend. Garlic, onion, peppers, herbs, spices, sausages and chicken. This hearty dish pairs lentils with tasty Italian sausages. The big difference between British and European sausages is in the curing. In Britain we would typically hang our sausages for 24 hours before eating them. In Europe, sausages might be hung for up to 12–14 days, allowing them to dry out and become firmer. They lend themselves to this type of dish.

200g brown or green lentils

75ml red wine

3 garlic cloves, peeled, 1 left whole, 2 chopped

salt and freshly ground pepper

4–8 Italian sausages, depending on appetites!

2 tbsp olive oil

½ red onion, finely chopped

1 celery stalk, finely sliced

5–6 sage leaves

2 tbsp tomato paste

Rinse the lentils and place in a pan. Cover generously with cold water, add in the red wine, the whole garlic clove and season with salt. Bring to the boil, reduce the heat and simmer uncovered for around 25–30 minutes. You want the lentils to be soft, but retain some texture. Drain the lentils, reserving their cooking liquid. Remove and discard the garlic clove.

Rub the sausages in olive oil before frying in a frying pan, over medium heat, turning now and then, until cooked through and nicely browned, probably about 20 minutes.

While the sausages are frying, heat the olive oil over medium-low heat in a heavy-based saucepan. Add in the onion, celery, garlic and sage leaves and fry over a low heat, stirring often, for 10 minutes, until softened and fragrant.

Add in the drained, cooked lentils, the tomato paste and 75ml of the reserved lentil liquid, and mix well. Cover the pan and cook over a low heat for 5 minutes, stirring now and then. Check the seasoning and adjust as required.

Serve the sausages with the lentils.

Paul's Burger

4 burgers

I have put my own name to this burger as I have strong opinions on the subject. A beef burger is minced and pressed beef. That's it. When you add chopped onions or bone marrow, or anything else, you are creating sausage meat. My other bugbear is the beef used. At Meat London we use only chuck steak, as it is full of flavour and contains enough fat to keep our burgers moist. I can't get along with people asking for portions of different cuts. It doesn't improve the taste.

Don't eat rare burgers! The Environmental Health have a good point here. If we take a piece of meat and it has bacteria on the outside, as it might, grilling to above 74^0C will kill the bacteria. If we take that same piece of meat and mince it, we mince the bacteria into the middle of the meat. Searing the outside won't kill the bacteria. Eating a rare or medium rare burger means you are taking a chance.

600g minced chuck steak

Light olive oil

Salt and freshly ground
    pepper

4 burger buns

4 beef tomato slices, 3–5mm

4 crisp fresh lettuce leaves

4 large gherkin slices

Divide the beef mince into four equal parts and loosely roll into balls. Press each ball carefully to form a patty 2cm thick at the most.

Heat a heavy bottomed pan, or a griddle, until it just starts to smoke. Rub each burger with olive oil and season with salt and pepper. Place onto the griddle and allow to sear for 90 seconds.

Turn the burger and leave for another 90 seconds. Do this twice more before removing from the pan and allowing to rest in a warm place.

Split the four burger buns and 'toast' in the cooking pan for about 30 seconds. Put the base of each bun on a plate and top with a burger. Put a piece of tomato, lettuce and gherkin on each burger. Top with the other half of the bun and serve while still hot.

Extras

Extras for burgers come in many guises and are all about individual taste. Good melting cheeses such as Emmental, Gruyere or Raclette are a joy. If you do want cheese, place a slice of it on top of the burger for the last minute of cooking. Bacon is another popular topping. Smoked streaky would be my choice. Personally, I don't think that a burger needs bone marrow but some people love it. Onion rings – raw or fried – also go down well.

The choice of sauces, relishes and chutneys is another way of adding variety. Have a look at p.77 for some of our favourites.

MORE BURGERS...

Having established that a 'real' burger is just meat, let's cheat for a moment and consider some other options...

Lamb and Mint Burger

600g minced lamb shoulder

1 tsp finely chopped fresh mint leaves

¼ tsp finely chopped fresh rosemary leaves

freshly ground pepper

Pork and Apple Burger

600g minced pork belly

100g cooking apple, peeled and chopped

1 pinch of ground cinnamon

Beef Chilli Burger

600g minced chuck steak

1 medium red chilli, finely chopped (de-seed the chilli, if you want it to be less hot)

1 tsp dark soy sauce

Freshly ground black pepper

Chicken and Herb Burger

600g minced chicken thigh meat

¼ tsp chopped fresh sage leaves

¼ tsp chopped fresh oregano leaves,

¼ tsp chopped fresh chives

BURGER SAUCES
AND RELISHES:

Spicy Tomato Ketchup

Makes approx 400ml

For the spice bag:

1 bay leaf

1 dried red chilli

1 garlic clove, peeled, left whole

1 tsp coriander seeds

4 cloves

600ml tomato passata

50g light brown sugar

75ml cider or white wine vinegar

1 tsp mustard powder

½–1 tsp chilli powder

½ tsp ground ginger

½ tsp ground black pepper

1 tsp salt

When it comes to burgers, tomato ketchup is an essential for many people. Making your own ketchup is very easy and satisfying and allows you to play with flavourings. This piquant, home-made ketchup packs a tangy punch. A great accompaniment for barbecued food.

Wrap the spice bag ingredients in a small piece of muslin and tie, forming a spice bag.

Place all the remaining ingredients, together with the spice bag, in a heavy-based saucepan. Stirring, gently heat through until sugar dissolved.

Simmer for 30–40 minutes, stirring now and then, until the sauce has reduced and thickened. Place in warm, sterilised bottles or jars, cool and store in the fridge. Use within 2 months.

Minted Cucumber Relish

Serves 8–10

300g cucumbers

1 shallot, very finely sliced

1 garlic clove, peeled, left whole

grated zest of ½ lemon

1 tsp salt

2 tbsp sugar

3 tbsp white wine vinegar

3 tbsp freshly chopped mint leaves

Mint and cucumber is such a good combination. Choose the small cucumbers – sometimes called Lebanese cucumbers – if you can find them as they have better texture and flavour. This quickly-made pickle – or 'quickle' – is a delightfully crunchy, refreshing relish. Serve it on the side with burgers or barbecued meat.

Slice the cucumbers as finely as you can. Place the cucumber, shallot, garlic and lemon zest in a bowl and mix in the salt. Cover and set aside for 2 hours.

Drain the cucumber mixture in a colander for 30 minutes and discard the garlic clove.

Place in a bowl and mix with sugar, vinegar and mint. Set aside for 30 minutes, before serving. Store in the fridge.

Salsa Verde

Salsa verde, meaning 'green sauce,' is a delicious, aromatic condiment for meat. The Italians classically serve salsa verde with bollito misto, boiled meat. It can also be used as a marinade or a dipping sauce. This is my version of this vibrant sauce.

It would be so easy just to throw all the ingredients into a kitchen aid, but where's the fun in that? Get a good knife. It takes time to chop finely with a knife, but it is an opportunity to practise your knife skills.

1 garlic clove, crushed

1 large shallot, finely chopped

3 anchovy fillets, chopped

2 tsp capers, drained and chopped

2 tbsp chopped flat leaf parsley,

2 tbsp chopped basil leaves

1 tbsp chopped mint leaves

1 tsp Dijon mustard

6 tbsp olive oil

1 tbsp freshly squeezed lemon juice

Freshly ground black pepper

Place the garlic, shallot, anchovies, capers, parsley, basil and mint inside a bowl.

Add the mustard and the oil and stir into a thick paste. The key is to remember that you want to achieve a thick, sauce like consistency. Stir in the lemon juice. Season with the black pepper. Don't be tempted to add salt as the capers and the anchovies are very salty.

This is a sauce that can be used at once but which will benefit from being left overnight in the fridge, so that the flavours combine and strengthen. Store in a glass or earthenware container, not a metallic one, as this will cause it to discolour.

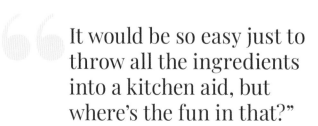

It would be so easy just to throw all the ingredients into a kitchen aid, but where's the fun in that?"

Makes approx 400ml

Mayonnaise

Without question, my favourite cold sauce will always be mayonnaise. I'm not sure if chips were invented for mayonnaise, or mayonnaise was invented for chips, but it is a heavenly combination. With such simple ingredients, it seems strange that making mayonnaise takes so much concentration, with the risk of curdling a sobering possibility. Be patient, relax and take your time. You could use an electric whisk, but please don't. Enjoy the pleasure of your sauce coming together under the steady beating of your balloon whisk.

2 very fresh egg yolks, at room temperature

1 tbsp Dijon mustard

Salt and freshly ground pepper

300ml groundnut oil

1 tbsp white wine vinegar, gently warmed on the stove or 1 tbsp freshly squeezed lemon juice, at room temperature

Place a good sized, clean bowl on a cloth or non-slip mat. Put in the egg yolks and mustard, mix together and season lightly with salt and pepper.

Whisking constantly, start to add the oil into the mix. You want to do this very slowly and gradually in a steady stream. Do not be tempted to take a slurp of wine.

As you whisk in the oil, the mixture will emulsify, becoming thick and creamy. Whisk it for 20 seconds more, then whisk either the warmed vinegar or lemon juice, to loosen the mayonnaise slightly. Taste and adjust the seasoning to your own taste.

It really is that straightforward. However, if the mix splits, you will get a curdled mess. Don't panic. Place another egg yolk in a clean bowl. Drizzle the curdled mayonnaise into this yolk, whisking vigorously all the time. The magic will happen.

Mayonnaise is so versatile. Simply by changing the oil to 50% olive oil, for example, the flavour will become completely different. If you want to give your guests the 'luxury' version, whisk in two tablespoons of double cream at the end. There's nothing to say you can't use a different mustard or add a spoonful of freshly chopped herbs. Once you've mastered the technique, let your imagination run wild.

GRILLING AND FRYING:
OFFAL

Serves 4

Fegato Alla Veneziana

Me and my mum both love veal liver. The rest of the family? No. In all of my years in the business, it's the one thing that mum always asks me to get for her. It is a bit expensive and very few people eat it, so it can be difficult to come by, but we do stock it. In this Venetian dish, the onions, gently cooked so as to bring out their sweetness, are a perfect match. Close your eyes and think 'gondola ride'.

2tbsp olive oil

100g butter

2 medium white onions, finely sliced

Salt and freshly ground black pepper

4 slices veal liver, each 150g and ½ cm thick

1 tsp chopped parsley

1 tbsp lemon juice

Heat half the olive oil and half the butter in a heavy bottomed pan. Just as the butter melts, add the onion and stir well. Make sure that all of the onions are well coated in the oil and butter. Keep the pan on a low heat and let the onions cook until softened and translucent, around 15–20 minutes. Keep stirring. Don't let the onions over colour. Season with salt and pepper.

When the onions are cooked, tip them into a warmed holding dish and keep them somewhere warm.

Slice the liver into 'fingers'. Without cleaning the pan, add in the rest of the oil and butter and let it heat up. Look for the butter to start to foam and carefully lay the liver into the pan. Let it cook for 2 or 3 minutes, stirring all the time, while turning the liver, in order for it to cook evenly on both sides.

Add the onions back into the pan to warm up. Mix in the chopped parsley and the lemon juice. Season to taste.

Serve by sharing the liver and onion mix evenly amongst four warm plates.

I love spaghetti and a small pile of plain spaghetti on the side of the plate, in order to mop up the juices from the liver, is a favourite of mine. Sauté potatoes, spinach or even a simple fresh tomato salad work well too.

Serves 4

Devilled Lamb Kidneys on Toast

Many customers never choose offal. It's strange because their parents and grandparents would have eaten and enjoyed plenty in their time. When cooked well, offal is delicious and it is generally inexpensive and has positive health benefits. Now, I must admit that brains are one of two foods that I really can't bring myself to put in my mouth. The other being rice pudding. So, no rationale there. This simple recipe offers a different option for breakfast or a good starter option for a dinner party.

1 tbsp Worcestershire sauce

1 tbsp tomato purée

1 tsp English mustard

1 pinch smoked paprika

1 tbsp lemon juice

1 tbsp butter

1 tsp olive oil

12 lamb kidneys, fat and skin removed, quartered with the core taken out

Salt and freshly ground pepper

4 slices brioche bread, lightly toasted

In a bowl, mix together the Worcestershire sauce, tomato purée, mustard, paprika and lemon juice.

Heat the butter and olive oil in a large frying pan. As the butter starts to froth, tip the kidneys into the pan and make sure that they are completely coated in the butter and oil. Season well with salt and pepper. Keep the kidney moving and cook for 3 minutes.

Tip the fried kidneys into the Worcestershire sauce mixture and stir to coat them well. Now, pour everything back into the pan and fry briefly – around 2 minutes – until the kidneys are cooked through.

Have the freshly toasted brioche slices ready in the middle of four warm plates and top each slice with a portion of the devilled kidneys. A final twist of black pepper and off to the table.

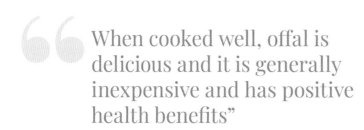

" When cooked well, offal is delicious and it is generally inexpensive and has positive health benefits"

Serves 4

Lebanese-style Chicken Livers

Chicken livers are one of those great pieces which people seem to forget about. They're affordable and have a lovely rich taste, which contrasts so nicely here with sour-sweet pomegranate molasses. The secret to this Lebanese mezze dish is not to overcook the livers, so as to keep them soft and moist. Serve with some good bread to mop up those tasty juices.

500g chicken livers

2 tbsp olive oil

½ red onion, finely chopped

2 garlic cloves, chopped

salt and freshly ground pepper

¼ tsp ground allspice

juice of ½ lemon

1 tbsp pomegranate molasses

2–3 tbsp pomegranate seeds

2 tsp chopped flat-leaf parsley

Cut the livers in half and trim off the fatty, stringy parts. Pat dry with kitchen paper.

Heat the olive oil over medium heat in a large, heavy bottomed frying pan. Add in the onion and garlic and fry, stirring, for 2 minutes, until fragrant.

Add in the chicken liver and fry for 2 minutes, stirring constantly to ensure they colour on all sides. Once all the livers have lost their raw look, season with salt and allspice. Pour over the lemon juice and pomegranate molasses, mixing well. Cook, stirring, for a further 1–2 minutes until the sauce bubbles.

Sprinkle with pomegranate seeds and parsley. Season well with freshly ground pepper. Serve at once.

BARBECUING

Barbecuing

The cooking method that happily shouts 'summer' and 'outdoor living'. Even in the British climate! So much fun and so few rules. Long sunny days with friends and relatives, too much beer, not enough sunblock and dad insisting that he was born to cook. Sausages and burgers, obviously. Lamb chops and chicken breasts for those wanting to spend a little more money, and fish and spit roast for the more adventurous. Tables groaning under colourful salads, bread, dips and sauces completing a fantastic day in the garden.

In recent years, Britons have embraced their barbecues with great passion and demand for new barbecue dishes is relentless. This gives the butcher an opportunity to shine, to use some imagination and to display otherwise untapped skills in championing cuts and marinades that work well on the barbecue. It's just so much fun for everybody. By the way, I used not to be a fan of the barbecue. However, a couple of years back I acquired a barbecue through our relationship with Weber-Stephen and I cooked my Sunday chicken on the spit. The 2kg bird took 90 minutes to cook and I was converted forever. The best chicken I ever had.

The term 'barbecue' refers to both the method of cooking and the equipment itself. In reality, it can also refer to the social gathering that ensues as people come together to enjoy the results. If you enjoy barbecuing it's worth investing in something longer term. Modern day technology means there are some truly splendid barbecues. They come in all shapes and sizes and can even be colour co-ordinated.

So where to start?

Gas or charcoal is one of the first things to think about. The advantage of gas is cleanliness and speed. A good gas barbecue can be up and running in a few minutes and will cook cleanly and efficiently for as long as the gas lasts. A gas machine works well for those who want to barbecue a lot, or for those cooking smaller amounts quickly and easily and, when it comes to controlling temperatures, they are certainly easier to use. The purist, however, would always argue that a 'real' barbecue uses charcoal. While I understand the benefits of gas, purely for flavour, for me, charcoal wins every time. There are two main types of charcoal: lump wood, which is cheaper, and briquettes. Lump wood is made from reclaimed wood; it burns more quickly but also gets hotter. Briquettes, on the other hand, are a compressed version of lump wood and last for much longer. Nowadays, one can find ethically sourced, sustainable charcoal briquettes.

Investing enough time in heating the coals is important. Using a fire lighter and piling the coals in the centre of the barbecue takes about 20 minutes. The coal will smoke initially but that dies down. The general rule of thumb is that the coals should be 'white hot' before you start cooking on them. Be aware though that as charcoal heats from the bottom, by the time the coals on the top are white hot

the ones at the bottom are losing their usefulness. To rectify this, a 'fire starter' is a useful and affordable piece of kit. It is an aluminium tube that holds the coal. As the top coals start to turn white, the fire starter can be tipped bringing the hot coals from the bottom to the top of the pile. These hot coals can then be poured onto the barbecue as needed.

The next question, is do you want to cook by direct or indirect heat? As a rule of thumb, anything that cooks quickly – such as a steak, a pork chop or lamb rump – would be cooked by the direct heat method. This is placing the burning charcoal in the middle of the barbecue and putting the food directly above. This way the food cooks quickly at a hotter temperature. Indirect heat is used for slower cooking and spit roasting. The hot briquettes are arranged around the sides of the barbecue and continue to burn as the meat cooks slowly and gently. A good quantity of briquettes will offer heat at around 200°C for about two hours. Sausages, for example, benefit from being cooked over indirect heat as strong heat threatens to burst their skins.

My spit roast prong for the barbecue is my new best friend. It was an investment to buy in the first place, but I'm glad I did. The open flames and the smoke from good quality charcoal or briquettes adds delicious flavours to the joint. A whole chicken, a leg or shoulder of lamb or pork neck are just a treat. A 2kg chicken over charcoal takes about 2 hours and is worth the wait. For the really adventurous looking to feed a crowd, spit roasting a whole lamb or pig is a commitment to time and effort, but why not? A 20kg lamb will take around 7 hours, so you'll have to be up early to get lunch ready. If you don't want to buy a spit roaster that big, they can be hired at a reasonable cost.

The deeper we get into using the barbecue, the more complex it can become, but the greater the results. A ten-hour beef brisket or an eight-hour pork shoulder for pulled pork, always a

winner. Even the average Christmas turkey will cook in about three hours. If the barbecue starts to lose heat, simply add more hot coals. One of the most important lessons to learn when barbecuing is that of leaving the food to cook. With modern, covered barbecues, if the meat needs a specific time to cook, it should be left untouched, apart from occasional basting. If you continually lift the barbecue lid the heat escapes and the cooking becomes erratic.

The other great use of a barbecue is for smoking meat. Adding soaked wood chips to the charcoal creates a delicious, pungent smoke that infuses the meat in the early stages of the cooking process. It's important not to forget to soak the wood well, as this will prevent the wood igniting quickly and helps produce the smoke. You can also create aromatic smoke by soaking and barbecuing woody stemmed herbs such as rosemary, bay or thyme.

Practically any meat can be cooked on the barbecue. A great, simple way to add flavour is to use spice or herb rubs and marinades. Chicken thighs, pork belly, lamb shoulder skewers and beef steaks are all popular cuts. Beer-Can Chicken (see recipe p.127) is a favourite as is Spatchcock Chicken, not forgetting, of course, that classic – the good old burger (see recipe p.72).

At Meat London we run a number of courses including our popular barbecue ones teaching barbecue skills and techniques. Every course covers a number of cooking methods and the appropriate meat. Dishes we teach include seasoned pork ribs (always a winner), chicken leg 'lollipops', lamb rump za'atar, classic sirloin steak and low, slow smoked beef brisket in Coca Cola. Sides, too, including picante potato wedges or spit-roasted vegetables. Our favourite grill chef Craig shares his in-depth knowledge on how to get the best from your barbecue and his endless enthusiasm ensures that nobody goes home hungry, thirsty or uneducated in barbecue skills.

BARBECUING:
BEEF

Korean Chilli Beef Short Ribs

This simple but effective marinade uses gochujang, the powerful, but mellow Korean chilli paste. These succulent beef short ribs cooked long and slow on the barbecue are a truly tasty treat – packing a great garlicky-chilli kick. Slow cooking suits fattier and tougher cuts of meat – the shoulder, belly, brisket and ribs to name a few. The long gentle cooking breaks down fat and sinews and intensifies the flavour of the meat. Serve with a crunchy white cabbage side-salad.

1.5kg beef short ribs in one piece

For the marinade:
4 garlic cloves, crushed
1 heaped tbsp gochujang (Korean chilli paste)
4 tbsp dark soy sauce
1 tbsp sesame oil
1 tsp sugar
1 tbsp oil

Using a sharp knife, cut small incisions into the flesh of the beef short ribs to help the marinade penetrate.

Mix together all the marinade ingredients. Coat the beef ribs well in the marinade. Cover and chill for at least 4 hours, ideally overnight.

Okay. We want to cook our short ribs for 8–12 hours over a low heat (110˚–130˚). If you are using gas, set your barbecue to 120˚C and you can now go for a beer while I explain how to use charcoal. If you are using charcoal, read on. The way we do this is to set the barbecue charcoal in a snake, or minion, pattern. Slowly and carefully lay the briquettes, one after the other, three quarters of the way around the base of the barbecue. You will need two rows wide and two high. You then light 5–6 briquettes and add them to the front of the pile, and off it goes. Over time, the first will light the second, and so on for many hours. Genius!

Put a container of some type – a foil dish would work well – in the middle of the barbecue and pour in some cold water. Now put the grate in place and lay the short ribs on the grate, bone side down. The water will keep the beef moist and the beef juices are going to collect in the container. Every hour, it's a good idea to 'spritz', or spray, or splash, the beef with liquid. Water or beef stock is good for this.

You want the beef to reach 95˚ at the centre. The bones will be loose when tugged. When the meat is cooked, it can be cut in between the bones and placed into the juices that have collected in the container. Cover with foil and allow to rest for 30 minutes before serving.

Serves 4

Beef Satay with Peanut Dipping Sauce

750g lean beef rump, cut into 6cm x 1cm strips

4 lime wedges, to serve

Skewers, for threading

Satay Marinade:

1 tbsp grated fresh ginger

4 garlic cloves, crushed

1 large shallot, finely chopped

4 tbsp brown sugar

3 tbsp fish sauce

3 tbsp dark soy sauce

2 tbsp vegetable oil

2 tbsp chopped fresh coriander

1tbsp ground cumin

½ tsp turmeric powder

½ tsp cayenne pepper

1 stick lemongrass – tough outer layers removed and discarded, white part bruised and chopped

Peanut Dipping Sauce:

150g smooth peanut butter

3 tbsp dark soy sauce

1 tbsp golden syrup

½ red chilli, finely chopped or ½ tsp chilli paste

1 garlic clove, crushed (optional)

Warm water, to taste

The writing of this book never would have happened without the enthusiasm and encouragement of the delightful and talented Jenny. When we first began working on the project together, it soon became apparent that my training was very much French classics and Jenny was to bring the Asian influence. So, especially for Jenny, I have looked at recipes, messed about with ingredients and come up with this version of a Beef Satay as a tiny 'homage' to her.

Using a blender or a food processor, whizz all the marinade ingredients into a paste. If you want a bit of a chilli kick, mixing in a small sprinkling of dry chilli flakes won't do any harm. Transfer it to a good-sized bowl.

Add the beef strips to the marinade and mix it all together. Cover the bowl and marinate the beef in the fridge for at least 4 hours or overnight.

Before you cook the satay, prepare the peanut dipping sauce. Put all of the ingredients into a bowl and mix together to a paste. Add warm water a little at a time until you arrive at the consistency that you like. Set aside.

When you are ready to cook the satay, remove the marinated beef from the fridge and divide it onto your chosen skewers. I have been purposely vague about the skewers. One can buy wooden or metal skewers in a variety lengths. I have allowed 175g of meat per person. This would fit onto one 12" skewer or 2–3 cocktail skewers. If using wooden skewers, soak them for 20 minutes beforehand as this helps to stop them burning when you cook the satay.

If you are going to cook the skewers on the barbecue, place them onto a non-direct heat and let them cook for two minutes before turning them and allowing another two minutes. They can be cooked in a frying pan or skillet in the same fashion.

If you want to cook them in the oven, place the skewers in a single layer in an oven tray. Preheat the oven to 200˚C. Cook the satay in the oven for 5 minutes, before turning and cooking for another 5 minutes.

Serve the freshly cooked satay with the peanut dipping sauce and a wedge of lime.

Serves 4

Six Hour Ox Cheeks

Ox cheeks are at the less expensive end of the scale, so I've been generous with quantities here. Cooking ox cheeks slowly on the barbecue is a real treat. We used beer from the Lost and Grounded beer brewery because we sell it and like it, but choose your own favourite ale. It will do the same job.

1 tbsp smoked paprika

1 tbsp freshly ground pepper

1 tbsp sea salt

4 ox cheeks, 1.2kg–1.5kg with any excess fat removed, along with any silver skin or sinews. Ask your butcher to prepare the cheeks.

200 ml brown stock (see p.266)

1 x 440ml can beer

Prepare your barbecue for indirect cooking at a very low heat, about 125°C.

Mix the paprika, pepper and salt in a dish big enough to take an ox cheek. Rub each ox cheek in the mix, ensuring that they are all well-seasoned. If you have a spray bottle, pour the beef stock into the bottle. If you don't have a spray bottle, baste the ox cheeks using a spoon.

Once the barbecue is hot enough, place your ox cheeks in carefully, ensuring that they are away from the direct heat. The action of spraying your food on the barbecue is called 'spritzing'. Spritz or baste your ox cheeks with the stock and pull the lid down. The cheeks are going to cook for around 3½ hours, until a dark crust forms on each cheek. Spritz or baste the cheeks every hour or so, during this period.

Transfer the cheeks into a heatproof dish and pour in the beer around them. You can add in any remaining stock from the spritz bottle. Cover the dish with two layers of foil and seal as well as possible. Place this dish back in the barbecue to cook for a further 2 hours, or until the cheeks offer no resistance when pierced with a sharp knife. If you use your probe, you should achieve 95°C.

When you are happy that the ox cheeks are cooked, remove them from the heat and allow to rest for 30 minutes in the cooking dish.

In my opinion, the best way to eat the ox cheek is in a brioche burger bun with a sliced pickled wally and a good helping of coleslaw (p.275).

Lamb Souvlaki

Everywhere we go in the world, we come across amazing street food. It always evokes a love for that country. The Greek 'souvlaki' literally translated means 'skewer', a reference to the way the meat is cooked. It's generally accepted that a souvlaki on the street will be wrapped in pitta bread with a yoghurt dressing. For many years, I supplied a fabulous Greek restaurant in London and the owner showed me how to make souvlaki. He used to insist that from Easter to October – the lamb season – he would only use lamb and from October to Easter he would only use pork. I hope this recipe doesn't let my Greek friends down.

Serves 4

600g diced leg of lamb

1 tbsp olive oil

½ red onion, finely sliced

2 medium tomatoes, thinly sliced

For the marinade:

1 tbsp olive oil
  1 tsp finely chopped fresh or dried oregano

1 garlic clove, crushed

¼ tsp cumin powder

1 tbsp lemon juice

Freshly ground black pepper

Tzatziki:

1 small cucumber, Lebanese if possible

Sea salt

1 garlic clove, crushed

1 tbsp olive oil

1 tsp chopped fresh mint leaves

4 tbsp natural Greek yoghurt

Flatbread: (You can buy pitta, but this is fun. Have a go)

300g self-raising flour

300g natural Greek yoghurt

Sea salt

First, marinate the lamb. Combine all of the lamb marinade ingredients in a large bowl. Add in the lamb and mix well. Cover the bowl with cling film and set aside for at least 2 hours or overnight.

For the tzatziki, peel the cucumber and de-seed it by cutting the cucumber in half lengthways and drawing a teaspoon down the middle. Finely slice across making small half-moon pieces. Place the cucumber in a strainer and sprinkle generously with sea salt. Stand the strainer over a bowl for 10–15 minutes so that the liquid will drain out. When ready, dry the cucumber in a clean towel. Tip it into a good size bowl. In another small bowl, mix the garlic and olive oil together and give it a through stir or whisk. Now add it to the cucumber with all of the other ingredients. Mix everything together and chill until needed.

When you are ready to eat the souvlaki, get the lamb out of the fridge and give it a stir. Thread the marinated lamb onto four barbecue skewers and set aside.

For the flatbread, mix the flour and the yoghurt together with a good pinch of sea salt and mix until the dough comes together and starts to leave the side of the bowl. Turn the dough out onto a lightly floured surface and knead the dough until it becomes smooth and a little elastic. Divide the dough into four equal pieces and, with your rolling pin, roll each piece in to a round disc about 25cm. Heat a heavy frying pan on the stove until it is hot and, one at a time, cook the flatbreads on one side for about 2 minutes before turning to cook on the other side. As each flatbread is cooked, wrap it in a warm cloth to keep it warm and moist.

Heat a tbsp of olive oil in your pan and cook your skewers for one minute on each side. This will get them to about medium cooked, a little pink in the middle. Let them rest in a warm place.

Lay a warm flatbread on your surface and put some red onion, tomato and a good dollop of tzatziki in the centre of each. Remove the lamb from the skewer and place it on top. Wrap the flatbread tightly around it. Repeat the process until all four flatbreads have been filled. Traditionally – and sensibly – the souvlaki would be wrapped in greaseproof paper or tin foil to be eaten. Keep a napkin handy and mind your best t-shirt.

Lamb Tagliata

'Tagliata' simply means 'cut' in Italian and this simple but stylish dish is a restaurant classic in Italy. It's usually made with beef steak, but, as I am very partial to lamb, I couldn't resist trying this riff. The lamb neck fillet is ideal for fast, direct cooking. I think it works. Give it a go.

1 garlic clove

salt and freshly ground pepper

1 tsp finely chopped rosemary leaves

3 tbsp olive oil

2 pieces of lamb neck fillet, each 300g

sea salt crystals, for sprinkling

a generous handful of rocket leaves

Parmesan shavings, to serve

balsamic vinegar, for drizzling

4 lemon wedges, to serve

Peel the garlic and crush it with a pinch of salt to a paste. Mix this with the rosemary and 2 tbsp olive oil.

Spread this flavoured oil over the lamb neck fillets, coating well. Season generously with freshly ground pepper. Cover and set aside at room temperature for 30 minutes.

Get the charcoal hot and set it under the cooking grate, in the middle of your barbecue. When ready, give the lamb one last rub with the oil and carefully lay it across the cooking grate. Close the lid of the barbecue, but don't go too far away. Let the lamb cook for 3 minutes and turn it over. Close the lid for another 3 minutes. Note: closing the lid of the barbecue stops flames shooting up, thus preventing the meat getting blackened.

Remove the meat from the barbecue and let it rest for 5 minutes.

Cut the barbecued lamb across into 1cm–thick slices. Place the slices in a serving dish. Sprinkle over a good pinch of sea salt crystals. Scatter over the rocket and Parmesan. Drizzle with balsamic vinegar and the remaining olive oil. Serve at once with lemon wedges on the side.

Spit-Roast Smoked Lamb Shoulder

Serves 6–8 people

Who doesn't enjoy a bit of 'one upmanship'?! That moment when your friends arrive at your barbecue and exclaim excitedly "what is that?" as the intoxicating smell takes over the garden. A boned and rolled lamb shoulder on the spit, with a handful of wood chips, will do it every time. If you ask your butcher to de-bone the shoulder, you should be able to do the rest yourself. If the thought of stringing the joint fills you with dread, take your marinade to the butchers and ask them to do it for you. You do need a spit on your barbecue. If it doesn't come with one, they can usually be added as an attachment.

4–6 sage leaves

2 tsp thyme leaves

4–6 mint leaves

1 tsp rosemary leaves

2 tbsp olive oil, plus a little extra for rubbing

salt and freshly ground pepper

a 2kg lamb shoulder, de-boned and beaten a little to flatten it out

Get your barbecue set for cooking with the indirect method (see p.91) to 200˚C and the spit ready.

Soak two handfuls of wood chunks in cold water. Put them directly onto the flames just before bringing the meat to the heat. The wood will smoke, and the lamb will absorb the smoke for the first 10–15 minutes of cooking.

Start by chopping the sage, thyme, mint and rosemary finely. Mix the chopped herbs with the olive oil, seasoning well with salt and pepper. Ideally, rest this for at least one hour in order for the flavours to blend.

Lay your shoulder of lamb, skin side down, on a flat surface. Spread the meat as widely as possible and, using a sharp knife, cut 3–4mm incisions, in a diamond pattern, across the meat. Rub the scored meat liberally with the herb mixture until the whole surface has a good coating.

Roll the shoulder as tightly as possible and secure with butcher's twine (well worth investing in some as it will come in handy again and again). The butchers knot always impresses our customers in the shops. There are any number of ways of doing it, but none make the meat taste any better. Tie your knots any way you can.

Push the rod from your spit through the lamb and secure it. Rub the outside of the lamb with any remaining marinade and put it onto the barbecue. Place a container under the meat to catch dripping fat. Close the lid and do something else. Let the lamb shoulder cook for 1½ hours. It is worth basting the meat once or twice during cooking, using the drippings from the lamb, but don't be tempted to lift the top more than necessary.

After 1½ hours, check the lamb to see if it is cooked. You want 75°C at core temperature. If you need to leave the lamb for a few more minutes, then do. It won't overcook. When you are happy that the lamb shoulder is ready, remove it from the barbecue and carefully remove the spit.

Put the lamb in the container that has been collecting drippings, baste with the juices and let it rest somewhere warm for 15 minutes. Carve and enjoy. You'll find that the smoking stage at the beginning of cooking has created a red ring around the edge of the lamb – the sign of triumph.

Craig's Pulled Pork

Serves 8–12

A number of years back, a young man called Craig married my niece. The family took an instant liking to him and he seemed a capable chap. So, despite the fact that he had no food background, I offered him a job at Meat London. I gave him the task of running our in-house Barbecue Courses and developing Meat London Events. Well, he's done a marvellous job and his cooking skills have come on leaps and bounds. He is such an amiable guy and our customers love his courses. Here we have his favourite Pulled Pork recipe. The round joint from the shoulder of the pig – also known as the Boston Butt – is fantastic for this job and big enough to keep the family fed at the annual summer barbecue. Bear in mind this recipe takes 3-6 hours.

2.5kg–3kg Boston butt, boneless and skinless, but fat on

8 hickory wood chunks

330ml cider

For the rub:

1 tbsp brown sugar

1 tsp smoked paprika

½ tsp cayenne pepper

½ tsp ground cumin

1 garlic clove, crushed or ½ tsp garlic powder

Set the barbecue for indirect cooking to 135°C.

In a clean bowl, mix all of the rub ingredients together. Put the pork in a large roasting dish, suitable for your barbecue. A purpose made 'Dutch oven' is perfect for this, but a tin roasting dish is also suitable. Rub the pork all over with the rub.

Add 8 wood chunks to the charcoal on the barbecue. I like to use hickory, but choose your own wood. The wood will smoke and infuse the pork for the first hour. Pour the cider into the pan with the pork and put the meat onto the barbecue. Pull the cover over the barbecue and leave it to cook for an hour, basting it after half an hour.

Now, baste the pork once again with the liquid from the pan. If your pan has a lid, cover it. If not, cover the pork with foil. You want a tight fitting cover. Return the meat to the barbecue and cook for another 3 hours.

Use your probe to check the temperature of the pork. The pork is cooked through when it reaches a temperature of 95°C in the middle of the joint. The pork might be ready after 3 hours, or it might need to cook some more. Use your probe to check for doneness every 30 minutes.

When you are happy that your Boston butt is cooked, remove the pan from the barbecue to a stable base. The pan will be full of juices. I recommend that you leave them all in the pan, but if you want to remove some of the liquid fat, you can. Pull the pork apart using two forks, so that it has a shredded appearance. Mix the meat with the juices in the pan, and you're good to go.

Serve the pork in a brioche burger bun with a good helping of BBQ Sauce. And why not try our fresh tasting Cucumber Relish (p.77) or our colourful Coleslaw (p.275)?

Stacked Sticky Pork Ribs

Who doesn't like sticky pork ribs? What's a barbecue without hot, meaty pork ribs in a tangy barbecue sauce or a spicy chutney? Mostly we sell the ribs from the belly. They're bigger and have more meat, but some people prefer the baby back ribs from the loin. On either style, there's a thin membrane on the concave side of the bones. Learn how to remove it, as you get a much more tender finish, or you could ask your butcher to do it. We always serve ribs on our barbecue courses and Craig has got this one down to a fine art.

2 sets of pork belly ribs cut in half, about 2kg

For the rub:

3 tbsp brown sugar

2 tbsp smoked paprika

2 tbsp ground cumin

2 tbsp English mustard

2 tbsp fresh coriander, finely chopped

1 tbsp dried chilli flakes

1 tbsp cracked black pepper

In a bowl large enough to take the ribs, toss all the rub ingredients in together and mix them well. Cover the bowl with cling film and let it rest for an hour or so. You could do this job a day in advance if you were so minded.

Get your barbecue set for non-direct cooking at about 150°C.

Rub the ribs all over with the dry rub. Stack the ribs, one on top of the other, in the middle of your barbecue, with the bone side facing down. Ensure that your ribs are away from the direct heat. Put the top down and allow to cook for 15 minutes. Now, take the ribs on the bottom of the stack, and move them to the top. Lid down again, and cook for another 15 minutes. Do this every 15 minutes until each rack of ribs has had 15 minutes on the bottom. Remove the ribs from the barbecue and put the top down to keep the barbecue warm.

Wrap the stack of ribs in two layers of foil and put it back onto the barbecue for another 2 hours, still away from the direct heat.

Remove the foil-wrapped ribs from the barbecue and unwrap carefully. At this stage, you can cut up the ribs and eat them as they are. You can also offer them to your guests with sauces and condiments such as the BBQ Sauce (p.110), the Spicy Tomato Ketchup (p.77), or even the Chimichurri (p.147).

As always, don't forget the wet-wipes.

Pork Belly Strips with a Cracking BBQ Sauce

Serves 4

The tangy, pungent aromas of a good barbecue sauce tantalises the nostrils. The combination of sweet and sour with a little chilli kick never lets us down. It's one of those dishes that is scent-led. You just know it is going to be delicious. I have paired it here with the pork belly, because why not? But once you have the sauce, it can be used for anything.

8 pork belly strips, each 100g, bone in

Salt and freshly ground pepper

BBQ Sauce:

2 tbsp rapeseed oil

2 shallots, finely chopped

4cm ginger, peeled and finely chopped

3 garlic cloves, crushed

1 tbsp ground allspice

1 tbsp smoked paprika

2 tsp mustard powder

1 tsp cayenne pepper

450g muscovado sugar

4 tbsp golden syrup

1 x 700g jar passata

250ml cider vinegar

2 tbsp Worcestershire sauce

Set the barbecue for indirect cooking to around 150˚C.

Rub the pork belly strips with salt and pepper and place on the barbecue away from the heat. Put a drip tray underneath the pork. Bring the top down on your barbecue and cook for 1 hour. After 30 minutes, turn the ribs over.

Meanwhile, back at the stove, make the BBQ sauce. Heat the oil in a large, heavy bottomed pot. Fry the shallots, ginger and garlic for a few minutes, stirring, until softened. Add the allspice, paprika, mustard, and cayenne pepper. Stir well for another minute. Control the heat so that the pan doesn't get too hot.

Whisk together the muscovado sugar and golden syrup, then add to the pot. Keep stirring and cook for 30 seconds.

Finally, add in the passata, vinegar and Worcestershire sauce. Give it all a good stir and allow to simmer gently for 10–15 minutes. Keep your eye on the sauce. Allow it to thicken, but not too much. Remove the sauce from the heat.

After the pork strips have been in the barbecue for an hour, prepare to cook them with the sauce. Lay out a piece of tin foil on the kitchen counter big enough to cover the strips. Lay a piece of baking paper on the foil and place the pork ribs on top in a single layer. Generously baste the pork ribs all over with the BBQ sauce and seal them well in the paper and foil. The paper inside the foil will help prevent the pork from burning. Put the pack back into the barbecue and allow the pork belly ribs to cook for another 1½ hours.

Bring the BBQ sauce back to a simmer. Remove the pork from the barbecue. Allow the package to rest for five minutes and carefully open the paper. As you open the package, there will be hot steam, so do be very careful. Place the pork belly ribs on a serving platter and baste them again with the BBQ sauce before serving. There should be enough BBQ sauce left to offer more to your guests if they want it.

Pork

When it comes to cooking and eating, the pig is really the most versatile of animals. No wonder pork is the most widely eaten meat in the world. From the pig we get bacon and sausages and ham. Also, pork chops, pork shoulders for the Sunday roast, spare ribs for the barbecue, succulent belly pork... Crackling, of course, is a joy. Having said that, I look to keep outer fat at not more than 20% of any cut.

At Meat London we find that a healthy pig weighing between 60–70kg and around six months old gives a good balance between fat and lean meat. While there are historic pig breeds in Britain – Tamworth, Gloucester Old Spot, Berkshire and Saddleback – like all the meat we use, our most important criteria is that the animal must have led a good life. Free-ranging in the open air, exposed to the elements and naturally fed. For many years now our pigs have come from a farm on the South Downs. They are born there and live on the land until they go to slaughter. Unlike cows or sheep, we use pig carcasses fresh, without the need to age or hang them.

Leg

A typical leg weighs around 12–15kg. A lean piece, it can be used in a number of ways. Hams, both cooked and cured –come from the leg. For British ham or gammon the hock will be removed at the first joint. For air-dried hams, such as Italy's prosciutto di Parma or Spain's jamon Serrano, the hock and bones are left intact. The cut of meat is salted to help preserve it and cured for between 12 and 36 months. If the meat is to be roasted, the leg can either have the bone removed or simply cut through and tied to create. The outer skin is scored and used to create fantastic crackling (for those who have teeth strong enough). From a butcher's perspective, the leg can also be separated into individual muscles – topside, the thick and the silverside. The leg muscles lend themselves to steaks for grilling or breadcrumbing, to be pan fried, but they are also tender enough for skewers or to use diced in stews. Right at the top, the rump, or chump, connects the leg to the loin and is a useful joint in its own right, again, good for steaks, but also a delicious roast.

Loin

The loin, or saddle, splits down the vertebrae to give two long round sections, each about a metre long. Depending on the butcher, when breaking down the pig, the chump might be left on the leg, but it is sometimes left on the loin and would be removed as part of the preparation of the loin. The pork fillet, sometimes known as the tenderloin, is the meat on the inside of the bone, from the chump to halfway along the loin. It is always soft and tender. The loin is ideal for chops, and the end with the fillet can be cut through to make the porcine equivalent of the beef T-Bone. Towards the end of the fillet sits the kidney and older readers will know that a pork chop with the kidney attached is a thing of beauty. Unfortunately, the health zealots scuppered that many years ago . . . The other end of the loin has the rib bones, hence loin chops (the same bones that become baby back ribs). It's a matter of debate whether the loin is better suited to chops or a roast. Removing the bones from the loin, scoring the skin and tying the joint into a roll gives us the perfect piece for roast pork. Just add apples.

Belly

The 'rags to riches' cut of the butchery world. Twenty years ago pork belly was a cheap cut. More often minced for sausages than given much time on a decent menu. So, what happened? Celebrity chefs. That's what. And, on this occasion, we should all be grateful. Butchers sat back and watched the cut's popularity – and its price – rise. Never forget, meat is a commodity and as more and more people wanted to eat it, belly became more and more valuable. At one time, a pork loin might have been 25% more expensive than belly, but not today. The two are often very close to parity. A slow roasted belly on the bone, especially on the BBQ, is so delicious. Slicing between the bones makes belly chops. Its mixture of fat and lean really does make the belly perfect for minced pork dishes, including sausages.

Shoulder

From the shoulder we get the cut we call the 'hand'. There is not much use for the 'arm' piece of the hand. Mostly, this would be de-boned for mincemeat. The upper part is good to dice, but the jewel of the shoulder is the inner part, which forms part of the neck. The shoulder is split through the ball joint to create a large, rugby ball-shaped piece, often known as the Boston Butt. Weighing around 3kg, this is a fantastic joint for spit roasting on the barbecue. A real winner for a family gathering. This, too, can be divided into smaller pieces and is ideal for dicing and sausages.

Pigs Cheeks

Another modern favourite. Food trends are led by chefs and these days one sees jowls and cheeks are making an appearance on many a fine menu. The great chef Fergus Henderson has been a real champion of nose to tail eating at St John's restaurant and many a good chef has followed suit

Trotters and Head

Europeans, especially the French, are masters at turning the trotter into a delicious charcuterie item. Boned, stuffed and cooked slowly, the trotter becomes a masterpiece. Chefs traditionally demanded the back trotter, as they are bigger and meatier, but the front trotter is just as good in the hands. The head, too, has its place. Cut into pieces and cooked in simmering water until the meat and fat fall off of the bone, the end product can be turned in terrines, with brawn a traditional British luxury. Whilst some people might wrinkle their noses at the thought of these less familiar cuts, if they actually tasted trotters or brawn I think they'd be pleasantly surprised.

Serves 4

'Echine' of Pork
with Smoked Paprika Butter

The 'echine', or shoulder of pork, is a joint which I learned about at the beginning of my career in Paris. The neck-end section of the pork shoulder (often called the 'Boston Butt') is a versatile joint, delicious cooked either slowly in the oven or spit roasted on the barbecue. In this recipe, we take the rib bones closest to the shoulder – the bottom section of the neck-end – and create pork neck chops. These are a lovely cut for the barbecue

2 tbsp vegetable oil

Salt and freshly ground black pepper

4 pork neck chops, each 200g

200g smoked paprika butter (see p.38), softened to room temperature

Get the barbecue started and set it for direct heat cooking. The temperature needs to be up to 200˚C.

Put the vegetable oil in a shallow dish and season well with salt and pepper. Put the pork chops into the seasoned oil, making sure that they are well coated.

Lay the chops directly over the heat of the barbecue and allow them to cook for 1 minute before turning for another minute.

Remove the chops from the heat and baste them well with the smoked paprika butter. Return them back to the barbecue, but this time, away from the direct heat, to cook by the indirect heat method. Put the lid down on the barbecue and leave for twenty minutes.

When the chops are cooked, remove to a serving platter and baste again with the smoked paprika butter before serving.

A Pair of Pork Skewers

This way of cooking meat is tasty and versatile. You can experiment with marinades, types of meat and the other ingredients threaded on the skewers. Pork, with its natural fattiness, is a great tasty meat to use. Skewers can be cooked in the oven or in a frying pan, but, for me, you can't beat cooking them on barbecue.

Makes 4

Pork Chorizo Skewers

400g pork leg, cut into 16 even-sized cubes

4 chorizo sausages

For the marinade:

1 tbsp honey

1 tsp wholegrain mustard

1 tsp chopped fresh oregano or ½ tsp dried oregano

1 tbsp olive oil

In a large bowl, mix the marinade ingredients together. Add in the pork cubes and coat well with the marinade. Cover and marinate in the fridge for at least 1 hour or overnight. The longer the meat marinates the better.

Cut each chorizo sausage into 3 equal piece. Take 4 long skewers. Alternately thread a pork cube, then a piece of chorizo, until each skewer has 4 pieces of pork and 3 pieces of chorizo.

To cook on the barbecue, see the advice below.

Pork with Pineapple Skewers

3 tbsp Jack Daniels (any bourbon will work)

½ tsp brown sugar

1 drop vanilla extract

12 x 3cm chunks of fresh pineapple

1 tbsp olive oil

½ tsp fennel seeds

Freshly ground black pepper

400g pork leg, cut into 16 even-sized cubes

Mix together the Jack Daniels, brown sugar and vanilla extract. Add in the pineapple cubes and mix to coat well. Cover and marinate in the fridge for at least 1 hour or ideally overnight. The longer the pineapple is in the marinade the better.

In a separate bowl, mix together the olive oil and fennel seeds, adding a twist of black pepper. Mix in the pork cubes, coating well, and marinate in the fridge for at least 1 hour or overnight if possible.

Take 4 long skewers. Alternately thread a pork cube, then a pineapple chunk, until each skewer has 4 pieces of pork and 3 pieces of pineapple.

To cook on the barbecue, see the advice below:

Set the barbecue to 200˚C, using the direct heat method.

Place the skewers directly over the heat and allow them to cook for 1½ minutes. Turn the skewers over and cook for another 1½ minutes. Repeat the process, cooking the kebabs for 6 minutes in total.

Putting the top of the barbecue down will assist the cooking process and prevent shooting flames.

Once cooked, remove the skewers from the barbecue and allow them to rest for 2 minutes, before serving to your hungry guests.

BARBECUING:
POULTRY AND GAME

Serves 4

Ginger-Soy Chicken Thighs

Chicken really is such a versatile bird and succulent thighs, in particular, are a great way to start your barbecue. This simple, Chinese-inspired marinade works a treat, adding flavour without overpowering the taste of the bird.

8 chicken thighs, skin on, bone in

salt

2 tsp runny honey, for brushing

1 tsp sesame seeds

For the marinade:

5cm root ginger, peeled and crushed

2 tbsp ginger wine or sherry

2 tbsp dark soy sauce

1 tbsp oil

½ tsp sugar

Season the chicken thighs lightly with salt. Mix together the marinade ingredients.

Make one or two shallow incisions into the top of the thighs so that the marinade can penetrate the meat. Coat the chicken thighs with the marinade, covering well. Cover and marinate in the fridge for 2 hours.

Set the barbecue to over 200°C (220°C max), and prepare it for indirect cooking. You want the barbecue to be hot enough to crisp up the skin nicely. Carefully lay the thighs skin side down, away from the heat, and close the lid of the barbecue.

Cook the thighs for at least 25 minutes. Check that they are cooked right through, using a meat probe to check that they are at least 75°C in the middle. Turn the thighs over and baste the crispy skin with the runny honey. Sprinkle with sesame seeds.

Serve the chicken on a warm platter, with good finger wipes.

Garlic Lemon Chicken

A nicely cooked piece of chicken fresh off the barbecue is hard to resist. This recipe uses classic Italian flavourings – they're classic for good reason.

4 chicken supremes, skin on

salt

For the marinade:

2 plump garlic cloves, crushed

grated zest and juice of 1 lemon

2 rosemary sprigs, leaves picked off

1 tsp coarsely ground black peppercorns

2 tbsp olive oil

Season the chicken with salt. Mix together the marinade ingredients. Coat the chicken supremes thoroughly with the marinade and marinate in the fridge for 2 hours.

When it's time to eat, take the chicken out of the fridge and turn it once more in the marinade.

Heat your barbecue for the direct cooking method to 180°C.

Lay the chicken supremes, skin side-down, directly over the heat. Close the lid of your barbecue and allow it to cook for 5 minutes. After 5 minutes, be ready with your tongs. Don't keep the top up too long, as you will be losing heat.

Turn the chicken over and cook for 20 minutes away from the direct heat. After 20 minutes, put your temperature probe into the middle of the thickest part of the chicken. You want it to be at least 75°C. Remove the chicken from the barbecue and allow it to rest for five minutes in a warm place.

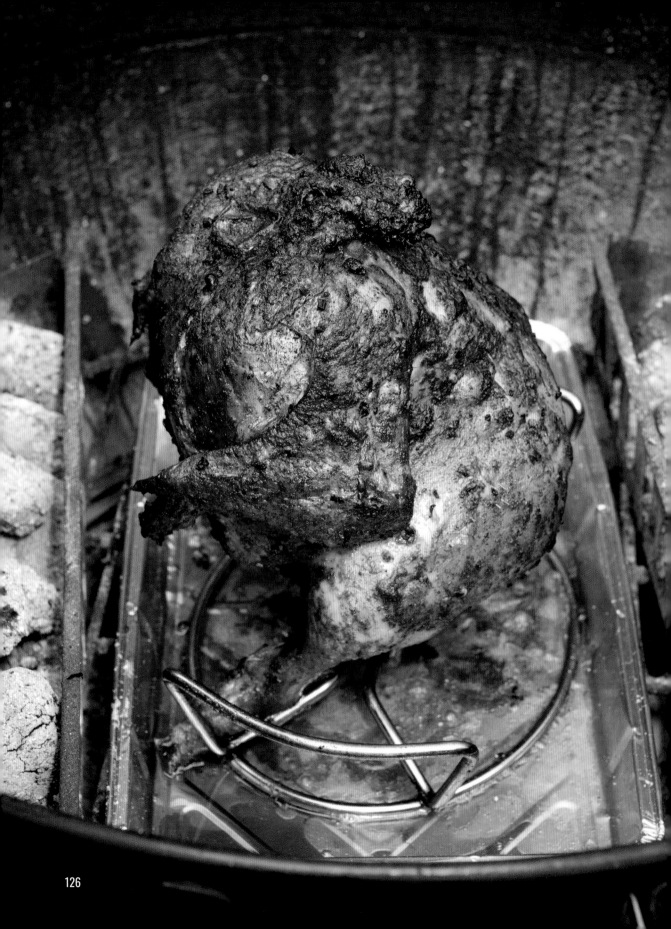

Saffron Beer Can Chicken

Serves 4

Pub quizzers will already know that saffron, kilogram for kilogram, is the most expensive spice in the world. Yet, because of its intensity, you need so little to make a difference that it becomes affordable. I wish I could claim the same for white truffles, caviar or even champagne, all of which I love. Was I born with such expensive taste, or did I just get lucky? This indulgent recipe justifies my fondness for the good things in life. For this, you are going to need a poultry roaster. You will also need a poultry roaster cup. Although an empty tin can will also work (Craig can sell you both).

½g saffron

1 tbsp warm milk

50g butter, softened

¼ tsp pink peppercorns

¼ tsp black peppercorns

½ tsp sea salt

1 free range chicken, 2 kg, wish-bone removed. Ask the butcher to keep the neck skin intact

1 tbsp olive oil

150ml glass of champagne (I feel bad – sparkling wine will also do the trick)

Soak the saffron in the warm milk. When the milk has cooled, put the butter into a clean bowl and add the saffron milk. Mix with a rubber spatula until well combined.

In a pestle and mortar, crush the pink and black peppercorns and salt. You need this mixture to be relatively fine.

Take the chicken and insert the saffron butter under the skin covering the breast. Spread the saffron butter as far as you can, but be very careful not to break the skin. Pull the neck skin over the cavity and then rub the whole chicken with the oil. Now rub the whole chicken with the pepper and salt mix.

Fill the poultry roaster cup or tin can with the champagne, and secure it into the poultry roaster. Put your chicken onto the poultry roaster. Make sure that it is sitting well, and stable. At this stage, you could stand the poultry roaster into a roasting dish of some type and spread some potatoes* around the base of the chicken. They are going to cook beautifully.

The barbecue should be set at 180°C for indirect cooking, and it will take about an hour and a half to cook, using about ⅔ of a chimney starter or three good handfuls of briquettes. If using a gas barbecue, set it to 180°C. Put the chicken into the middle of the barbecue, with the top down, for an hour and a half. Use your temperature probe to ensure that the chicken has reached 75°C at the thickest part.

Carefully lift the chicken away from the barbecue and allow to rest for 15 minutes. I like to joint the chicken into pieces and let my guests serve themselves.

*Chop some thyme and rosemary and add a spoonful of rapeseed oil. Mix with a good portion of small potatoes and a sprinkling of sea salt.

A Day in the Life of Meat London

Running a shop well takes a lot of work and especially so when you sell food. At Meat London, we serve over 2000 customers every week, while dealing with around 50 suppliers, including farmers, producers, cheesemongers, wine suppliers and laundry companies. A lot of what we source and sell is British, but not all of it. Personally, I don't think a good deli section would be complete without international delicacies like Spanish chorizo, Italian Parma ham or Greek olives or wines from countries around the world.

Right from the start, we decided that Meat London would focus on selling to the public, instead of offering a wholesale service to hospitality. We wanted to concentrate on looking after our customers in the shops rather than supplying demanding chefs. Twice I went against my own rules and supplied restaurants. Each time they folded and we were left with unpaid debts, so now it's no restaurants. Because of this, we don't need to start work at silly times in the morning. We open from 9.30am and we close at 6pm. Our team have 30 minutes in the morning to get the shop set up and 30 minutes in the evening to clean and close down. It's all very simple.

Like everything else, making the job look easy is the greatest skill."

As the team start to arrive at about 8.45am, the coffee machine gurgles and hisses. Our machines and coffee come from local chap, Harry Sergio. Everyone keeps his number on speed-dial so that we never run out. By 9am the buzz starts, the fridges are turned on, the meat starts to arrive, and the counters have to be wiped over and filled, ready for opening. The team have an alarm set on an iPad to warn them when its opening time. The awning at the front is down, the dog bowl by the door filled with fresh water and the door is open.

Every member of the team has their own tasks. Everyone knows their role, but we still have a discussion each morning to sort out and prioritise the day's tasks. The butcher and deli teams have very different roles. The business is heavily fresh meat driven and the butchers start the week by clearing away anything left over from the previous week. The measure of our success can be seen in the waste bins. The lighter the bins, the better we are doing. By the way, it costs a small fortune to get the fat and bone taken away once a week. When I started in the industry many years ago, we used to get paid for the waste fat and bones, while the giblets from birds attracted a premium. Now, we pay over £100 per week to have it all taken away.

I digress, where was I? The sausage machine rarely gets a day off. By late morning, the guys will be making fresh sausages to get us through to the weekend. We make eight or nine varieties on a weekly basis, including our ever popular 'Stokey Pokey'. Once a year, we invite our customers to submit their own sausage recipes for consideration. The butchers make small batches of the practical suggestions and Craig cooks them off. The team taste and mark each sausage, and the top six make it through to the last round. Come the day of the final, we cook up huge batches of the six final sausages in cocktail form, and invite our customers to come and taste and vote for their favourite. It's a really popular event – the mulled wine flows and much fun is had. At 4pm, the voting box is whisked away for counting and the Meat N16 garden fills up in anticipation of the winner being announced. The winner is awarded the 'Stokey Pokey Cup' and given complimentary tickets to our 'Meat the Sausage Course'. And here's a thing – based on our customers' votes – the editor of this book, the delightful Jenny Linford, won it herself one year – a proud moment for her she tells me.

Meanwhile, back scenes, there is the seemingly never-ending process of cutting, chopping and marinating: making meat skewers, burgers, spatchcock chickens, chicken schnitzel and chimichurri steaks. It all starts on Tuesday and ends on Sunday lunchtime. The early part of the week sees aged beef being de-boned and packed ready for the week ahead and the busy weekend. Paddy brings our pork and some of the lamb from the farm on Wednesday and this gets cut, or 'broken', into its useable parts. We have a small poultry delivery on Tuesday morning, when the shop re-opens after Sunday, and more fresh poultry arrives in time for the weekend. By early on Friday, our meat fridges are bulging. The reason I use the phrase 'busy weekend' is that we do around sixty-five percent – sometimes even more, of our week's business between Friday and Sunday.

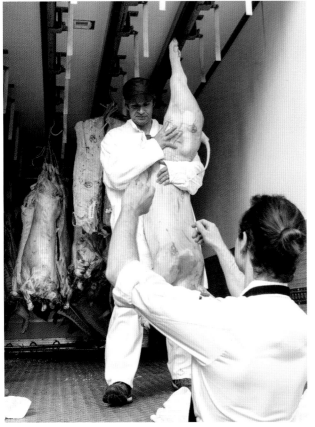

The deli side, too, requires looking after. There are always hams and salamis to be trimmed and kept in good condition, tubs of olives and pots of taramasalata or hummus to be filled up and cheeses to be cut and wrapped. As with the fresh meat, our deliveries are staggered to ensure that the products are at their absolute best for the customers. The deli team also look after dry goods and the selection of sauces, marinades, rubs, condiments and preserves.

We are also known for our wine rooms, with each shop stocking around 150 assorted whites, reds and roses, ports, beers and ciders. We match each wine to a relevant meat and on the weekends we do customer tastings, something our customers have come to enjoy. It is a little difficult to convince the butchers that when the deli team are sitting down to taste through the wines with the suppliers – with 10 or 12 bottles in front of them – that this is real work! Like everything else, making the job look easy is often the greatest skill. Our fabulous wine rooms don't happen by accident.

Another of our daily challenges is keeping the shops clean and safe. Working with fresh meat, this is a major responsibility. We understand how important it is that our fresh food must be kept properly chilled and handled properly. We use a food safety consultant to oversee what we do and guide us in good practice and legislation. We check the temperature of goods coming into the business and fresh product needs to find its way to the fridges as soon as possible after delivery, in order to maintain a cold chain. The fridges have their temperature taken three times every day to make sure that they are doing their job. Our teams spend time every day checking fridges, product date codes (shelf life) and packaging, and recording the results. From time to time, the local Environmental Health Officer will pop around, in order to check up on us.

Offering butchery-related courses and events is the third part of our business and this is something which the team and I very much enjoy. Our classes happen mainly at Meat

N16 where we have enough space, although we do hold tasting events at Meat NW5. They range from one-to-one butchery courses to hands-on group classes on beef, lamb, pork and chicken and our very popular barbecue courses. Holding these means that at any given time, as well as running busy shops, we can have a number of guests to look after, but we enjoy the challenge.

By 4pm each day, the first shift finishes. Everybody gets one early afternoon each week, but, before they go, the back of house is their responsibility. Scales, machines, tools, surfaces and floors need to be cleaned and sanitised ready for the evening and ready for the next day.

At 6pm, with a quick glance up and down the road for any straggling customers, the shop door closes, the awning goes back up and the dog bowl is put away. One last burst of activity sees the meat stored for the night, the blocks scraped, the slicing machine and scales scrubbed and the tools washed and

put away. The bins are emptied and new bags put in place, cardboard is tied and put out for collection and the floors are scrubbed and mopped. The cleaning is always done at the end of the day. Nothing is left dirty overnight.

Job done. By 6.30pm everybody finishes together. House rules dictate that everyone starts together, and everyone finishes together. Some break off for a quick cigarette, and on the weekend, we offer our teams a beer or glass of wine in the garden. Then it's time to change and go home.

Tomorrow, we get to do it all again.

ROASTING & BAKING

Roasting

I think that for many people the traditional Sunday roast is the most important meal of the week. It can be a meal for two, a meal to get the family around the table and a meal to share with friends. I can't imagine a time when the Sunday roast didn't feature in my weekend plans. I know from the time and care that they put into selecting the right joint, a lot of our customers feel the same way.

Roasting comes in various forms. There is the traditional roast in the oven, but the same oven can also permit a 'slow roast' at a lower temperature, taking a number of hours. Modern barbecues have the 'top down' option which simply moves your kitchen oven to the great outdoors (or garden, let's not get dramatic). Or does it? Are you going to roast on a gas barbecue or over charcoal? Will you throw a handful of wood chips on to add to the flavour? And let's not forget roasting a whole joint, or even a whole animal on a spit. In the Barbecue section (p.88), I explain how to roast using a barbecue.

Cookbooks, the Sunday glossies and TV chefs will all offer any number of hints and tips on to how best to roast your joint, but here's a thing – 180–200°C will suffice for most traditional roasts. One useful thing to do is spend a little time getting to know your own oven. The oven's size, age and cleanliness will all affect the heat and come into play a little.

That said, there are some tips and hints that might help. Nowadays, many recipes call for the joint to be started on a higher heat – 220°C for the first 30 minutes, with the heat then reduced to 180°C for the remainder of the cooking time. This starts the cooking process and then lets the heat penetrate the joint. One thing is for sure, once you have decided on your method, chosen your temperature and decided on the cooking time, don't open the oven door for any longer than you have to. Every time the door is opened, heat escapes.

For a traditional roast, cooking times vary according to the oven temperature, the size of the joint and to what degree you want the meat cooked. After many years, I have started to use a digital thermometer and, I will admit, it's the best £10 gadget I ever bought. It just makes life easier. However, you should still have a rough plan of your cooking time. All the good advice says 20 minutes per lb, plus 20 minutes (40 minutes per kg, plus 20 minutes). As a rule of thumb, you're not going to be far out. If you don't have a thermometer, it's the old-fashioned method for you: push a sharp knife or skewer into the meat and hold for the count of ten. Bring the knife to your bottom lip. If it's cold, your meat is still rare (or even raw). If it's warm, your meat is between rare and medium, and if the knife burns your lip, and you jump, then your meat is fully cooked. Take my advice; spend £10 on a digital thermometer.

If I've talked you into the thermometer, then these temperatures are good to know. Rare is at about 60°C, medium around 65°C and well done is 75°C. This is true for all meat and poultry. By the way, any bacteria in meat will die at 74°C. So, 74°C is definitely the safest option, if not always the tastiest.

Poultry should always be cooked to a minimum of 75°C. To test whether your bird is cooked, pierce the skin between the leg and the body and watch the juices run out. These must be a clear golden colour. If there is any sign of pink or blood give the bird another 10 minutes and try again.

The final stage of a traditional roast is to rest the meat or poultry. There's a good reason for doing this. It's a bit like running. When we run, we don't stop dead in our tracks. We slow down until we come to a stop, and it's the same for meat. It doesn't stop cooking the minute it is removed from the heat. During cooking, moistures inside the meat will be drawn towards the outside of the joint. By allowing the meat to rest, the juices inside cool and are re-absorbed, making the meat tender and succulent. By the time you come to cut,

or slice, your roast, the meat will be settled. Remove the joint or bird from the oven, carefully turn it upside down in the pan, which lets the juices run back through the meat, and cover loosely with foil. After 10 minutes, turn the meat up the right way again and leave to complete its 30 minutes' resting time.

Slow roasting at lower temperatures – around 140–160°C – can create amazing results with minimum effort. Invariably, the fattier, often cheaper cuts fare best. Pork belly, lamb shoulder, beef brisket all produce a delicious end result. A 5kg pork neck end (Boston Butt) or a 3kg beef brisket can be left to cook gently for 8 hours or more. A decent lamb shoulder or piece of pork belly will take around 3–4 hours. For poultry, larger birds can be slow roasted. Turkeys, geese, ducks and cockerel are ideal and would cook for a proportionate time to their size. With a slow roast you want to baste the meat often. Maybe every 15 minutes, after the first hour, remembering not to leave the oven door open too long. Usually a large joint is covered loosely with foil. This stops the top cooking too fast and burning or drying out. Slow roasting creates really tasty, earthy 'peasant' food in the best tradition.

Serves 4–6

Roast Beef Forerib with Marrow Bone Gravy

A most spectacular meal. Fantastic British beef, cooked on the bone with a gravy made from its own juices and enriched with marrow. Oh, and obviously, Yorkshire puddings on the side. Enough said!

Once you have committed to the expense of a delicious beef forerib roast, make sure that the butcher is giving you a fabulous piece of meat. The beef should be from free range, grass-fed cattle and been dry-aged for 25 days. Most butchers will French trim the top bones, but this is not critical. The base (chine) bone, however, should be sawn across – so it comes away after cooking and allows carving – then tied back onto the meat. When you cook the beef, it should be standing up, with the bones acting as a trivet, which is why it is often known as a 'standing' rib roast.

2 tbsp Dijon mustard

1 tsp chopped rosemary leaves

Salt and freshly ground black pepper

A 2-bone forerib of beef, 2–2.5kg

For the marrow bone gravy:

100ml Madeira

200ml beef stock

1 marrow bone, 1 shank around 600g, cut into 3 pieces

For the Yorkshire puddings:

115g plain flour

3 eggs

275ml milk

salt

dripping from the beef or vegetable oil

Preheat the oven to 240°C. You want it good and hot.

In a bowl, mix together the mustard and the rosemary and season with salt and pepper. Stand the beef in a roasting tin and carefully score the fat on the back. Don't cut the string attaching the meat to the chine bone. Rub the joint all over with the mustard mixture, making sure every bit is covered.

Put the beef into the middle of the oven and roast for 20 minutes. After 20 minutes, turn the oven down to 180°C and baste the rib with any juices that have appeared. Roast the beef for an hour more, basting it twice during that time. This will leave the beef cooked to around medium. If you want it rare, reduce the cooking time by 20 minutes. If you prefer the beef more cooked, roast it for another 20 minutes.

Remove from the oven onto a holding dish and loosely cover with foil. The beef is going to give off more juices, so make sure that there is some depth in your holding dish. Leave to rest.

The batter for the Yorkshire pudding needs to rest for at least 30 minutes, so, while the beef is cooking, get yourself ahead. In a clean bowl, whisk the flour, eggs and milk together, adding a good pinch of salt. Cover the bowl with cling film and leave the batter to rest until the beef is cooked. It doesn't need to be refrigerated.

Pour the beef juices from the roasting tray into a jug. As the liquid cools, the beef fat (dripping) will rise to the top. With a spoon, remove as much of the fat as possible to use for the Yorkshire Puddings.

As soon as the beef is out of the oven, increase the temperature to 220°C.

Using the dripping from cooking the beef, or a little vegetable oil if there is not enough, put a teaspoonful in each of the Yorkshire pudding moulds. I find a 12–hole tray works best. Put the Yorkshire pudding tray onto the middle shelf of the oven and allow it to become very hot.

Bring the tray out of the oven and pour the batter evenly into each hole. Return to the oven and get the door closed quickly, so as to retain the heat. The Yorkshire Puddings will cook for 20 minutes until they become well risen, crispy and golden brown. Don't be tempted to open the oven door. Light and airy Yorkshire puds don't appreciate temperature changes as they cook.

While the Yorkshires are baking, make the marrow bone gravy. Return the roasting tin to the stove and add in the Madeira. Scrape the bottom of the pan with a spatula to loosen the flavourful sediment and bring the Madeira to the boil. Add the stock and give a good stir.

When the stock boils, transfer it into a clean pot and add in the pieces of marrow bone. Allow the sauce to simmer gently. Slowly, as it cooks, the marrow will be released from the inside of the bones. After about 15 minutes, you will be able to remove the bones and, once they become cool enough to handle, you can tease out any remaining marrow into the liquid. Give a good stir. At this stage, pour the remaining cooking juices from the jug, plus any that have formed in the holding dish, into the pot. Stir well, bring to the boil and sieve into a clean pot. Simmer the sauce very gently until thick enough to coat the back of a spoon.

By now, it will be about time to remove the Yorkshire puddings from the oven. Take them out of the moulds onto a wire rack.

When it's time to serve, cut the strings on the rested forerib, give the chine bone to the very grateful dog (you could make a stock from the bones, but that's not going to please the dog) and lay the beef on your carving dish fat side up, so that it is resting on the tips of the bones. Arrange the Yorkshire puddings around the beef, pour your fabulous marrow bone gravy into a sauce boat and take it all to the table with a sharp carving knife and the satisfied smile of a good host.

Laura's Veal Rolle

The Italians are very fond of veal and Laura Feliziani, from our N16 shop, remembers this delicious recipe from her childhood back in Rome. Given its Italian origins, using an Italian air-cured ham such as Parma or San Daniele is appropriate, but any air-cured ham would work.

The eggs are soft-boiled, so need to be handled carefully, but the result is well worth it.

4 eggs

4 slices Parma ham

4 veal escalope, each around 100g, flattened to 0.5cm thickness

2 tbsp olive oil

butcher's twine, for tying

Preheat the oven to 180°C.

Bring a pan of water to the boil, add in the eggs, return to the boil and boil the eggs for six minutes. Remove the soft-boiled eggs from the heat and refresh under cold running water immediately, so as to stop the cooking process. Once the eggs are cool to the touch, shell them carefully.

Carefully roll each egg first in a slice of Parma ham, then wrap it in the escalope. Tie the 'parcel' with butcher's twine to keep everything together.

Place the veal bundles on a baking tray and brush liberally with olive oil. Bake in the oven for 15 minutes. Gently turn the bundles over and allow to cook for another 15 minutes. If the meat appears to be browning too quickly, loosely cover with foil.

Rare Roast Beef Topside

A good roast beef sandwich is a thing of beauty. I like to use a good, white bloomer, doorstep style, with salted butter and the beef well seasoned with black pepper. I'm not a huge mustard fan but sometimes I get the urge for a light covering of Dijon mustard. On the other hand, my mate here insists that a beef sandwich has to have a smattering of horseradish. When you want rare beef to use in a sandwich or a salad, choose beef topside. This is a muscle from the top of the leg which contains very little fat, and is best cooked rare. In fact, it becomes disappointingly dry if overcooked.

For a rare finish, work on 20 minutes per 500g of meat. Start with the oven a little higher and bring the temperature down; for rare roast beef, you don't want a crust on the surface of the meat.

Investing in a meat probe thermometer is a great help when trying to achieve a specific level of rareness. The beef will carry on cooking even after it's taken out of the oven, so these are the temperatures you're looking for.

> Rare: 55°– 60°C
> Medium: 60°– 70°C
> Well done: 70°– 75 °C

2 tbsp rapeseed or vegetable oil

Sea salt and freshly ground pepper and sea salt

1kg beef topside

Heat the oven to 220°C.

Pour the oil into a roasting tin and season the oil well with salt and pepper. Roll the beef in the oil, making sure that it's covered all over.

Put the tray with the beef in on the middle shelf in the oven and cook for 20 minutes.

Turn the oven down to 180°C and roast for a further 20 minutes.

Remove the beef from the oven, and lift it out of its juices onto a holding dish. Loosely cover it with foil and leave to rest in a warm place for 30 minutes.

Slice it thinly for sandwiches or salads. The beef will keep for 3–4 days in the fridge.

ROASTING AND BAKING: LAMB

Serves 4

Lamb Rump with Chimichurri

The lamb rump is at the top of the leg and is one of those cuts that often gets overlooked in the butcher's shop, if not by the chef. One lamb rump is a perfect mid-week roast for two but could also be sliced into small steaks. It's paired here with the piquant, Argentinian chimichurri sauce, which will have you doing a tango after dinner.

2 lamb rumps, each
    450g–500g

Chimichurri:

3 garlic cloves, peeled

2 good handfuls of flat-leafed
    parsley

1 tbsp chopped fresh
    coriander

2 tbsp fresh oregano leaves
    or 2 tsp dried oregano

3 tbsp red wine vinegar

8 tbsp olive oil

½–1 tsp red chilli flakes

Salt and freshly ground black
    pepper

Now, I could just tell you to whizz the herbs in your food processor until roughly chopped and then add the other chimichurri ingredients and blitz them again. But where's the fun in that?

Start by crushing the garlic, and putting it in a bowl. Now, using your trusty 12" chef's knife, get your heart pumping by chopping the parsley, coriander and the oregano (if using fresh) very fine indeed. Add the chopped herbs to the bowl with the garlic

Add the vinegar, olive oil and chilli and give it all a good stir. Let the sauce rest for five minutes, stir again and season with salt and pepper. Cover the sauce and leave it in the fridge for at least 4 hours. It will last in the fridge for up to 4 days.

Preheat the oven to 200⁰C. Using a sharp knife, score the skin side of your lamb rumps in a diagonal pattern. Rub salt and pepper into the meat. Heat your griddle or heavy bottomed pan until it just starts smoking. Put the rumps onto the griddle, skin side down. After a minute, the fat from the meat will start to render and the pan will crackle a little. After another minute, remove the pan from the heat and turn the meat over. The skin will have browned and crisped. Now baste the meat with the juices from the pan and cook it in the pre-heated oven for 30 minutes. This will leave the lamb rump quite rare. If you would prefer your lamb medium, give it 40 minutes. Remove it from the oven and leave it to rest for 15 minutes.

When you are ready to serve, slice the lamb as thinly as possible and place a decent portion on each of the warmed plates. Spoon a large dollop of chimichurri on the side and serve immediately. Put a small bowl of chimichurri on the table for those who just can't get enough.

> "There's something regal about roast lamb. To me, it conjures up everything that is good about British food and farming."

Roast Lamb

There's something regal about roast lamb. To me, it conjures up everything that is good about British food and farming. A Sunday roast with lamb is always a treat. Serve the meat with a few green vegetables, a crispy roast potato, the cooking juices from the roasting tin and there's heaven on your plate.

When it comes to roasting lamb, one conundrum is whether or not the joint is best cooked on or off the bone. There are merits to both. Many argue that meat cooked on the bone gains flavour from those bones. For me, the benefit of the flavour from the bone is outweighed by the value of the meat that is lost in carving from the bone. Certainly, the juices in the pan, from which you will want to make your gravy or sauce, will benefit from the bones and the marrow within, but there is no reason why these bones can't be added alongside the meat, or even used as a trivet for the joint to sit on.

When I was training as a chef (just after dinosaurs died out) most roasting joints would be 'sealed' in a hot pan until they were golden brown and caramelised all over, then roasted. The theory was that all the goodness and juices were being sealed inside the joint, however in 1984, the respected food scientist, Harold McGee, dispelled the theory as a myth. Today, many chefs rub the meat with oil and seasoning, or herbs, and many follow the trend for cutting slits in the joint and pushing in flavourings – popularly garlic and rosemary. The joint is then roasted in the oven to cook a little more slowly. Now, I'll happily throw my hat into the ring. I don't like lamb to be piqued with garlic or rosemary, or anything actually, when it's being roasted. The flavour of good roast lamb is so sublimely subtle that it doesn't benefit from anything – especially garlic – being pushed into its flesh.

Once the joint is cooked, do let it stand in a warm place, resting, for 20 to 30 minutes. The muscles will relax, the juices will stop bubbling away inside and the flavours will be enhanced. Once cooked, the tasty cooking juices can be used to create a delicious sauce or gravy. Likewise, add seasonings and flavours to vegetables and garnishes that will enhance the lamb. The other thing I don't do, is I don't season my joints with salt, as I feel this taints the natural juices before I start my sauce. There you are; each to their own.

Slow roasting, where the joint is cooked long and gently in the oven, produces delicious results with lamb. It's so simple as well. Just set the oven as low as you like - add the lamb - and let low heat and time work their magic. The art of good slow roasting is to have a good-sized joint surrounded with plenty of flavouring in the form of vegetables, herbs and spices. The larger joints (and small pieces don't lend themselves to slow roasting), should be loosely covered with foil at the start of the cooking process. Remember, too, that you need to baste the joint regularly during cooking. Pouring the cooking juices back over

the meat every 15–20 minutes keeps the joint juicy and flavourful. For myself, I cook traditional roasts off the bone and slow roasts on the bone

It's very difficult for the butcher when a customer asks: "how much do I need for 6 people?" There are so many considerations – people's appetites, second servings, other courses… However, as a rule of thumb, allowing around 200g per person of boneless meat and 300g per person of meat with the bone, will provide decent portions.

Serves 4

Crusted Lamb Rack

I've already mentioned that 'lamb chops' is the Latin for 'use your fingers'. It just is the best way to eat them. Get the butcher to 'chine' the rack; that is, saw through the bottom, vertebrae bone (or back-bone) and then tie it back into place. The purpose of this is to allow the rack to be roasted standing up, using the vertebrae as a natural trivet. When cooked, simply cut away the string holding the bone and slice the rack into individual cutlets.

1 x 8 bone rack of lamb, French trimmed and chined

1 tbsp Dijon mustard

For the crust:

1 tsp finely chopped flat-leafed parsley leaves

1 tsp finely chopped mint leaves

1 tsp finely chopped oregano leaves

3 tbsp fresh breadcrumbs

4 tbsp olive oil

salt and freshly ground pepper

To make the crust, mix together the parsley, mint and oregano. Add the breadcrumbs and mix well before adding enough olive oil to make the mixture resemble a dry-ish paste. Season with a little salt and pepper and leave to rest.

Preheat the oven to 220°C.

Heat a dry, heavy bottomed pan until the first sign of smoke. Place the lamb rack skin side down into the pan. Within a few seconds, the meat will start to sizzle and give off a little fat. It will take about 1 minute for the skin to brown. Remove the pan from the heat and let the lamb rack cool so that it can be handled.

Stand the lamb rack in a roasting tray, using the chine bone as a trivet to protect the meat from direct heat. Using a sharp knife, score the fat side of the rack, in a diamond pattern (making cuts not deeper than 2mm) and brush the Dijon mustard liberally over the whole piece. Now press the herb and breadcrumb mixture into the mustard, ensuring that the whole of the back is covered.

Roast the lamb in the oven for 30 minutes. Baste once during cooking with the juices from the pan. Remove from the oven and leave to rest for ten minutes in a warm place. The lamb rack will be cooked to medium.

When ready to serve, snip the twine holding the chine bone in place and carve the cutlets between the bones.

Serve with something simple. In summer, in the garden, a beautiful tomato salad would do the trick. At the dining table, maybe a selection of green veg. The lamb will be the star of the show.

Lamb Saddle with Caramelised Baby Onions and White Wine Jus

Serves 4

I make no secret of the fact that this is one of my favourite cuts. The saddle is from the middle of the animal and is all tender meat. Rolled properly, it looks so elegant and is a real winner for any dinner party. Adding the soft, sweet baby onions on the side is a bit like putting a silk hanky in your pocket before you leave the house. An unassuming touch of decadence.

2 tbsp olive oil

1 tsp finely chopped fresh herbs (I like thyme, rosemary and sage) or dried mixed herbs

salt and freshly ground pepper

1 kg lamb saddle, de-boned and rolled

For the caramelised baby onions:

28 baby onions, peeled

100g butter

1 tbsp sugar

For the white wine jus:

1 sprig of rosemary

100ml white wine

200ml lamb, veal or chicken stock

Preheat the oven to 230°C. Pour the olive oil into a flat dish and mix in the finely chopped herbs. Season with salt and pepper. Liberally rub the lamb with the mixture.

Place the lamb in a roasting tray and roast it in the preheated oven for 15 minutes. Reduce the heat to 180°C and roast for 30 minutes more. Remove from the oven and allow to stand in a warm place for a further 15 minutes. This will leave the lamb saddle pink in the middle. If you prefer your lamb a little more cooked, roast it in the oven for 45 minutes during the second period.

While the lamb is cooking, put the baby onions into a heavy-bottomed pan and barely cover with cold water. Add the butter and sugar and bring the pan to a brisk simmer. Stir the liquid from time to time and allow the water to evaporate. As the water evaporates, the butter and sugar will form a caramel, which, in turn, will coat the onions. Once all the water has gone, the onions will have become soft and almost translucent. Keep stirring the onions for about 1 minute to ensure that they are golden brown. Be careful at this stage to not let the onions burn. Remove from the heat and keep the onions warm in a side dish.

If you are confident of juggling your pots, the jus can be made once the lamb is rested. However, if having more than one pan on the go is a bit stressful, then keep the lamb and onions warm to one side. The jus doesn't take long.

Remove the lamb saddle from the oven pan and discard the excess fat and oil. Put the pan on a low heat and add the rosemary sprig. Stir it around for a few seconds until you can smell its odours. Pour in the white wine and mix well, while scraping the sediment from the bottom of the pan. Allow the wine to reduce by about 60%.

Now add the lamb stock to the pan and allow to simmer. if you don't have lamb stock, veal or chicken stock will be fine. Beef stock, though, will overpower your jus. Once the liquid has reduced by 50% it should be starting to thicken slightly. Cook it to the thickness you prefer and season with a little salt and pepper. Pour through a fine sieve into a warm jug. Some people finish the jus with a knob of butter before sieving, but I prefer not to make the jus too rich.

Slice the lamb saddle into 4 equal portions and place each on a warm plate. Pour a little of the jus onto the lamb and a spoonful of glazed baby onions on the side (I have allowed 7 onions per person. More or less doesn't change the recipe). Serve to your drooling guests.

Serves 4

Fragrant Za'atar Roasted Lamb Shoulder

Za'atar is a Middle Eastern blend of herbs that usually combines wild thyme, oregano, marjoram, and sesame seeds. In this dish, it forms the base of a marinade that works well with the fatty richness of a lamb shoulder, creating heady odours around the kitchen and a moist, tender meat. Serve with bulgur wheat or rice and lentils and an aubergine side-dish or enjoy slices of the lamb in a flatbread (see p.99) with chopped cucumber and tomato, sliced pickles and a dollop of tahini sauce. Happy smiles guaranteed.

½ a lamb shoulder

Marinade:
Juice of 1 lemon
Salt and freshly ground black pepper
1 garlic clove, crushed
3 tbsp zaa'tar
3 tbsp olive oil
2 tsp Aleppo chilli flakes

With a sharp knife, cut incisions into the lamb shoulder about 4mm deep, to allow the aromatic marinade to penetrate.

Mix together all of the marinade ingredients and rub it all over the lamb shoulder, covering it thoroughly. Place the lamb in a large dish and cover with cling-film. Marinate the meat in the fridge for 4–8 hours.

When you are ready to cook the shoulder, remove it from the fridge and allow it to come back to room temperature, around 30 minutes.

Pre-heat your oven to 200°C. Place the lamb on a rack in your roasting tray, loosely cover with foil and pop into the oven. Immediately lower the heat to 180°C and roast for 1 hour. Remove and reserve the foil and cook the lamb for another hour, basting with the marinade and meat juices every 15 minutes to keep it moist.

When the lamb is cooked, remove from the oven, re-cover with the foil and allow it to rest for 30 minutes before carving.

Tandoori Roast Leg of Lamb

I love the idea of getting 'stuck in'. Rubbing marinades into large joints of meat is a simple but effective way of adding flavours to it. This Indian-inspired Tandoori leg of lamb – cooked in the oven or in a covered barbecue – makes a splendid centrepiece. For maximum flavour, marinate the lamb a day ahead of cooking it. Serve it with naan bread or basmati rice, a crisp-textured salad and a cucumber raita for a feast.

1 leg of lamb, 2kg, bone-in

Marinade:
2 tbsp white wine vinegar

2 tsp salt

6 cardamom pods

6 tbsp natural yoghurt

1 tsp ground turmeric

1 tsp chilli powder

1 tbsp ground coriander

2 garlic cloves, peeled and pounded

1 thumb size piece of root ginger, peeled and pounded

A handful of fresh mint leaves, pounded

With the point of a sharp knife, cut slashes over the leg of lamb to about 3mm deep. This will allow the marinade to penetrate the meat fully. Place the lamb in a large dish or non-reactive tray. Mix together the vinegar and salt and rub the mixture liberally all over the leg. Cover the dish and put the whole dish into a fridge for at least half an hour to let this penetrate and do its work.

Crack the cardamom pods, extract the seeds and grind them well in a pestle and mortar. Crushing with a rolling pin will do just as well. Now mix the cardamom with the remaining marinade ingredients to make a paste. Remove the lamb from the fridge and rub the yoghurt mixture all over the leg, massaging it into every slash made previously. Re-cover the dish and put it back into the fridge to rest for at least 4 hours, turning the lamb in the marinade once or twice. Overnight will be even better.

When you're ready to cook the lamb, remove it from the fridge and transfer it to a roasting tin. Leave the lamb to sit until it comes back to room temperature, around 30 minutes.

Preheat the oven to 200°C and cook for 1 hour 40 minutes. As it roasts, baste the meat now and then with the cooking juices. If the lamb looks like it is browning too much, loosely cover it with tin foil.

Once the lamb is cooked, remove it from the oven and let it rest, with a loose covering, in a warm place, for 30 minutes before carving.

ROASTING AND BAKING:
PORK

Cider Roast Pork Belly with Caramelised Apples

Pork belly was once overlooked but now that chefs and food writers have discovered its joys it's become very popular. Rightly so. By its nature, it is a fatty cut, but much of the fat comes out through the cooking process and it is always succulent and full of flavour. In my opinion, the pork belly benefits from being cooked on the bone. The bones will impart extra flavours and, once the belly is cooked, the bones can be pulled away easily.

½ tsp fennel seeds

½ tsp black peppercorns

1 tsp smoked paprika

1kg piece of pork belly

1 tbsp rapeseed oil

1 medium carrot, chopped

1 medium onion, chopped

1 celery stalk, chopped

4 sage leave

1 star anise

3 apples (the apples need to be firm. Braeburn or Granny Smiths should do the job)

30g butter

2 tbsp maple syrup

250ml dry cider

1 heaped tsp plain flour

Using a pestle or mortar or a rolling pin, crush together the fennel seeds, peppercorns and paprika.

Carefully score the skin of the pork belly with a sharp knife (a Stanley knife works well for this). Lay the pork on your work surface skin side down and rub two-thirds of your fennel seed rub all over the meat. Turn the meat over again and place it in a roasting tray. Let the pork rest in the fridge for 1–2 hours to absorb the flavours from the rub.

Preheat the oven at 180˚C. Remove the pork belly from the fridge and pat away any moisture from the skin. Rub the rest of the fennel and paprika mix into the skin with the rapeseed oil. Add the chopped carrot, onion, celery, sage and star anise to the roasting tin. Pour 250ml cold water around the pork, but do not allow the water to touch the skin of the pork as this would prevent the skin from crisping up. Roast in the middle of the oven for 1½ hours.

While the pork is in the oven, cut each apple into 8 wedges, Remove the core, but do not peel. Melt the butter in a heavy bottomed pan until the foam is just dying down. Lower the heat and add the apple wedges. Turn the apple slices so they become covered in the butter and allow to cook for a minute. Now add the maple syrup and again, turn the apples so that they are coated in it. Turn the apples constantly until they take on a rich, golden colour. Remove from the heat and keep warm.

After 1½ hours, the pork should be soft enough for a knife to go through easily and the bones should be falling away from the meat. Boost the heat to 220˚C. Pour the cider into the roasting tin and cook the pork for another 15 minutes. The skin should now be a golden brown and crisped up. Remove from the oven and allow to rest for 20 minutes.

Carefully lift the pork belly onto a holding dish. Pull away the bones. Loosely cover the meat with foil and keep to one side.

To make the sauce, first scrape the bottom of the roasting tray to get as much as possible of the goodness. Sieve the contents of the roasting tray into a clean saucepan, discarding the flavourings. With a spoon, remove as much of the fat as possible from the top of the liquid. Reserve the fat and use it for cooking potatoes or eggs or a confit.

Place the flour in a small bowl. Gradually add in the roasting pan juices one spoonful at time, whisking well so as not to allow any lumps to form. Once all the juices have been added, pour it back into the pan and bring to the boil. Allow to simmer gently until the sauce reaches a good consistency.

To serve, cut the pork belly into 4 equal pieces. Use your artistic license to decide on strips or squares. Place a portion on each of four warm plates and spoon the cider sauce over the top. Finally, spoon a share of the caramelised apple onto each piece of pork and enjoy the applause from your guests.

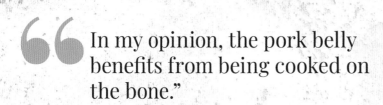

In my opinion, the pork belly benefits from being cooked on the bone.”

Country Terrine

I love the idea of a terrine for lunch, preferably with the end of a baguette or a slice from a good bloomer, a stick of salted celery, a pickled onion and definitely a few cornichons. A home-made terrine is also a great dinner party starter, as it can be made a couple of days in advance, giving you more time to chat to your guests.

700g minced pork shoulder or belly

200g smoked streaky bacon, finely chopped

1 tsp olive oil

1 knob of butter

1 large shallot, finely chopped

100g chicken livers

2 garlic cloves, crushed

½ tsp chopped thyme

75ml port

1 tsp chopped curly parsley

½ tsp ground mace

Salt and freshly ground pepper

10 slices of air-cured ham

Mix the minced pork and chopped bacon in a large bowl.

Heat the olive oil and butter in a pan and sweat off the shallot until it softens. Don't allow it to colour. Add the chicken livers, garlic and thyme and cook them together for 2–3 minutes. Keep stirring to ensure that the livers are well coloured all over, losing their raw appearance. Take the liver mix off of the heat and allow to cool completely.

Chop the livers roughly and add them, with the fried shallot, garlic and thyme, to the pork mixture. The livers may still be a little pink in the middle, but they will finish cooking with the rest of the terrine.

Add in the port, parsley and mace. Season with salt and pepper, bearing in mind the saltiness of the bacon and ham. My own preference is for a good amount of black pepper and less salt. Mix everything in the bowl very well. Cover with cling film and allow to sit for an hour or so in the fridge.

Preheat the oven to 160°C. Line a 1kg terrine mould with the air-cured ham, overlapping the slices slightly and allowing the ends to lie over the sides of the mould. Slowly and carefully fill the mould with the terrine mix. Make sure that the mix is pushed right into the corners and sides. Now fold the ends of the ham over the top of the mix. If your mould has a fitting lid, put it in place. If not, carefully cover the terrine with tin foil and pierce the foil once or twice.

Place the terrine dish in a roasting tin. Pour in hot water so that it reaches about half way up the mould, and cook in the oven for 11/2 hours. When cooked, the terrine should be at least 75°C in the middle, or an inserted knife should come out clean.

Allow the terrine to go cold before loosening all the way around the edge and tipping it out onto a cold plate. The terrine can be kept in the fridge for 2–3 days, but I bet you taste the first slice immediately!

Roast Pork Loin with Prunes

This is a classic French dish which I learned how to prepare during my time in Paris in the early 80's. It's possible to arrange the prunes in the pork so that, when the meat is sliced, they form the shape of a fleur de lys. I showed my dear friend Michael McGrath, who now works in our Meat NW5 shop, how to do this way back, when we both worked at Harvey Nichols. Today he prepares it better than me. I have simplified the method for this recipe, but it's none the less tasty. For this particular recipe, it is much better to remove the skin of the pork. Ask the butcher to remove the skin, but leave the fat in place.

800g pork loin, boneless and skin removed

12 pitted prunes, French Pruneaux d'Agen are ideal for this, but they are not always easy to come by, so use the best prunes you can find

salt and freshly ground pepper

100ml port

30g butter

Preheat the oven to 200˚C.

Lay the pork, fat side down, on your work surface. Open it so that the thick loin is closest to you and the flat side is facing away. Place the prunes one by one along the seam where the eye of the loin finishes. Roll the pork forward to form a nice cylindrical shape. Rest the joint so that the pork fat is facing upwards.

Using a very sharp knife such as a Stanley knife, create a diamond pattern in the fat by scoring it across at an angle at about 3cm apart and 4mm deep, then repeating the process the other way. Using butcher's twine, tie the pork at about 4cm intervals.
Sprinkle salt and pepper onto the fat and rub it in.

Put your pork into a roasting tray and roast it in the middle of the oven for 50 minutes. Pork is not a meat that should be cooked too rare. Use your meat probe to ensure that the centre of the joint gets to a least 70˚C before removing it from the oven.

Loosely cover the pork with foil and let it rest for 15 minutes. During the resting period, the pork will get to 75˚ at the centre while still being moist. Keep it warm until time to serve.

Cut nice thick slices, about 1cm each, and serve on a warm plate.

Remove any excess fat from the roasting tray and deglaze with the port on the hob. Allow the port to boil and reduce by half. Add in the butter and stir well. Spoon the juices over the meat to serve, alongside a bowl of buttered mange-tout.

"If you want to get into an argument with the Italians about the best way to make porchetta, good luck. This is how the boys at Meat London do it."

Porchetta (Aussie Rules)

One of our team comes from Rome and every time the boys mention or make porchetta, her eyes glaze over with excitement, or is it maybe memories of home? The physical making of porchetta is nearly as much fun as eating it. In Italy porchetta is often sold from food vans at markets, as street food – with slices carved off to order and placed inside a panino (bread roll). It is a dish you can also cook at home in the oven or on the barbecue. By nature of the piece of meat, it is very difficult to make a small porchetta. This recipe uses a 4kg piece here, but you could get away with a 2kg piece. Anyway, just invite your friends round for a porchetta party.

4kg pork middle – the loin and belly in one piece, de-boned and skin scored

For the seasoning:
1 level tbsp cracked black pepper

1 level tbsp fennel seeds

1 level tbsp chopped garlic

1 tsp chopped oregano

1 tsp chopped rosemary

1 tsp salt

In a bowl, mix all of the seasoning ingredients together. Lay the pork on your work surface, skin side down, and stretch it out. Sprinkle the seasoning evenly over the pork and get stuck in. Rub the seasoning all over the pork, ensuring that it all gets covered. From the loin side, tightly roll the pork, so that the belly is on the outside. Turn the pork onto the seam to stop it unrolling.

Use butcher's twine to tie the meat every 4cm to create a nice cylindrical shape. Don't worry about the knots, you're not applying for a job! Once the meat is tied, let it rest for at least an hour in the fridge. You can prepare it a day in advance and let the seasoning really get to work. You can then cook it either in the oven or the barbecue.

Let the oven warm up to its highest setting. Put the pork into a deep oven dish and place it in the centre of the oven. Immediately reduce the heat to 180^{0}C. Cook for 30 minutes, then baste the skin with the juices in the oven dish. Baste every 20 minutes or so for the next 3 hours. The skin will crackle and become a golden colour. If you think that the skin is burning, make a loose covering with aluminium foil.

When the porchetta is cooked through to at least 75^{0}C at its centre, remove it from the oven and let it rest for 30 minutes.

Or set your barbecue to 200^{0}C. If using charcoal, you should be using the 'indirect' method (see p.91). Attach the porchetta firmly to the spit and rub the outside with good cooking oil. Put the porchetta in place with a drip tray underneath, to catch the juices. Allow to rotate for at least 30 minutes, with the barbecue lid closed, before looking in and basting the pork. It will take between 2 and 3 hours to cook, and you should baste the meat with its juices every 30 minutes. The heat of the barbecue will diminish with cooking. If it falls below 150^{0}C, you add some more coals. Spit roasting takes a little more effort, but for flavour, it gets my vote

When the porchetta is cooked, let it rest for 30 minutes, find the ciabatta rolls and open a bottle of Sangiovese.

Chinese Honey-glazed Roast Pork

This classic Chinese way with pork really is a winner. The pork is first marinated, then roasted in the oven over a tray of water to keep it moist. The results are salty-sweet and quite irresistible. Serve it with steamed jasmine rice or egg noodles. Any leftovers work a treat in noodle soups or stir-fries.

2 pieces of pork fillet, each 400g

2 tbsp honey, for glazing

For the marinade:

1 garlic clove, crushed

1 tsp salt

4 tbsp soy sauce

4 tbsp sugar

1 tbsp rice wine or sherry

2 tbsp hoisin sauce

1 tsp Chinese five-spice powder

Cut diagonal slits at 4cm intervals on opposite sides along the pork fillets, cutting just three-quarters of the way through the fillets, but not all the way through. This allows the marinade to really penetrate the pork.

In a bowl large enough to hold the pork, mix all of the marinade ingredients together. Add in the meat and coat it well with the marinade. Cover and refrigerate overnight, turning over once or twice during that time.

Preheat the oven to 180°C. Pour boiling water into a roasting tray until it reaches about halfway up the sides. Place the marinated pork on a rack above the water, reserving the marinade.

Roast for 20 minutes, then brush the pork all over with the reserved marinade. Return the pork to the oven and roast for a further 30 minutes. Using your trusty probe, check that the meat has reached at least 75°C.

Remove the pork from the oven and brush the honey all over it while it's warm, making sure you glaze every bit. Serve it warm from the oven or at room temperature, carving it across into fine slices

Sausage Rolls

I do love a good sausage roll. They're easy to make and always go down a treat. The very idea of a warm sausage roll, fresh out of the oven, is enough to get me reaching for the mixing bowl. A big dollop of garlic mayo or a spoonful of spicy tomato ketchup and we're fit for the King.

A couple of things about sausage meat. First, we want to keep the meat quite coarse; I don't like soft, pappy sausage meat. It is possible to chop the meat by hand, but it's a bit long winded. I like to put sausage meat through the mincer only once. For most mince, we mince it twice, the first time breaks down the meat, and the second time blends the lean and the fat, but we are going to mix the sausage meat by hand, so let's not over mix it at the outset.

My other point is that I am not putting bread into my sausage meat, because we are going to eat the sausage rolls when they are freshly made. Bread, or rusk, gives longevity to the sausage meat, but we don't need it here. If you have to make sausage meat a day or two in advance, add 150g of bread, soaked in milk, to the recipes below. Of course, not everyone has a mincer in their tool box, so remember to tell the butcher what you want when buying mince for your sausage rolls.

I am offering two recipes here. Just for fun. The first, the Cumberland mix, is a traditional blend that has stood the test of time, and the second, the Argentinian Chorizo, was borne out of a customer request. A guy was doing some street food and asked if we would make him some sausages, so we did. Our customers liked them so much, we just keep making them. They will make a great addition to your party table.

Now, as you are getting used to me through the book, you'll know that I am all for doing everything from scratch, and by hand. But – to contradict myself on this occasion – I do use ready-made puff pastry for this recipe. Mostly because I make sausage rolls on a whim, and it takes 24 hours to make puff pastry. However, without doubt you will get a better result if you make your own and I have put a recipe on p.277 if you have the time and inclination.

Sausage Rolls

Makes six 10cm-long sausage rolls

Cumberland:

1kg pork neck or belly, minced

2 tsp finely chopped fresh sage

2 tsp – chopped fresh thyme

¼ tsp nutmeg

¼ tsp cayenne

¼ tsp mace

1 tsp salt

1½ tsp black pepper

500g puff pastry

1 egg, beaten, for egg wash

Argentinian Chorizo:

450g beef chuck steak, minced

450g pork neck or belly, minced

150g pancetta or smoked bacon, minced

2 tbsp smoked paprika

2 garlic cloves, crushed

100ml red wine

1 tsp freshly ground black pepper

½ tsp salt

500g puff pastry

1 egg, beaten, for egg wash

Whichever sausage meat filling you choose to make, the method remains the same.

Put all of the ingredients into a good-sized bowl. Mix well with one hand. It is important to ensure that the sausage meat is mixed well, otherwise, you will have pockets of ingredients in the finished sausage meat. Cover the bowl and leave to rest in the fridge for an hour or so.

Roll out the puff pastry to about 3mm thickness. It doesn't matter how long the piece is but it should be 12cm deep. Keep any offcuts of pastry, but don't roll them in a ball. Lay them out flat, one on top of the other. Then, the pastry can be re-rolled and rested to be used again.

Put the sausage meat into a piping bag with a 3cm nozzle, and pipe along the length of the rolled-out pastry closest to you. Using a pastry brush, paint a line of the egg wash on the opposite edge of the pastry. Roll the length of the pastry and sausage so that the two sides of the pastry join, with the inner pastry being sealed by the egg wash. Make sure that the seam is at the bottom of the sausage roll. This is to stop them opening during cooking.

Sausage rolls can be any size you want. With a clean, sharp knife, cut the individual sausage rolls to your chosen size, and carefully place them on a sheet of greaseproof paper, on a baking sheet. Leave adequate space between each sausage roll for the puff pastry to expand, maybe 5cm.

Put your baking tray in a fridge for 30 minutes. It is important not to let the sausage rolls warm up because the pastry would melt. Preheat the oven to 200⁰C.

Brush the chilled sausage rolls with the egg wash; this will make them turn golden brown in the oven. If you want a decorative finish, draw the back of a pointed knife in lines across the sausage rolls three times.

Bake the sausage rolls for 30 minutes. Don't be tempted to open the oven door during cooking; pastry doesn't like changes in oven temperature as it cooks. Remove the baking tray and carefully lift the sausage rolls onto a wire rack to cool down.

Paul & team,
Meat London, NW5

The arrival of Meat NW5 on Fortess Road, the humble row of shops near where I live, changed my life. Don't laugh! I'm not exaggerating. Meat NW5 opened its doors when my children were 3 and 1 and my days went like this: "cook, clear up, cook, clear up, cook, clear up". What we were going to eat and when was the pivot around which my life circled, endlessly. And my family are the fussiest eaters in North London, which as you can imagine, is quite the achievement.

It was a pretty lonely life, chained as I was to the whim of couple of mad toddlers and a husband who would only eat grass-fed, hand-reared, sunshine-filled genuinely happy animals. But Meat NW5 and, more important, Gessica, Michael and Ryan, Freddie and Sam made it all so easy. A delight, even. Suddenly I could buy 200g, and no more, of beef mince for a child's cottage pie; there were elegant Merguez for an echt Southern French couscous recipe; there were pre-marinated BBQ ribs, which we decided were not just for summertime. There was hand-cut British ham that was so honest and fresh that it was often the headline star of a weekend lunch.

But Meat NW5 is more than just a shop. In our increasingly atomised society, any local place where you are recognised, greeted as a friend and treated as a regular, is a tremendous luxury. Meat NW5 is intwined in our little community, now. It's as vital as the pavements, the trees and the streetlights. If it ever leaves, I will simply have to go with it.

Esther Coren

ROASTING AND BAKING:
POULTRY AND GAME

Chicken Cordon Bleu

Serves 4

Anything with melting cheese is delicious. The aroma gets the taste buds jumping even before the eyes can see it, and Cordon Bleu is no different. A classic recipe would probably ask for a good Emmental cheese, but here is an opportunity to experiment and give your own slant to an ageless classic. Reblochon is my cheese of choice today, but what about Raclette or Gruyere? Or – if you want to go out on a limb – maybe a blue cheese?

4 chicken fillets

4 slices cooked ham, cut at No3 on the machine

1 Reblochon cheese, diced

75g flour

3 eggs, beaten

100g panko breadcrumbs

2 tbsp vegetable oil

50g butter

Preheat the oven to 180˚.

Lay a chicken fillet on your board and cut into the middle of the fillet from the long side, but without cutting all the way through. When opened, the breast should look vaguely heart-shaped. Place the chicken between two pieces of cling film, and tap it flat with a rolling pin. The chicken will not need to be beaten a lot or too hard. You could use the palm of your hand.

When the four fillets are ready, lay a slice of ham onto each one. Then divide the cheese between the chicken, on top of the ham. Fold the chicken over, as if making a sandwich. The chicken fillets will now resemble their original shape.

Carefully roll the chicken in the flour, making sure that it is completely covered. Pat off any excess flour. Dip the chicken into the beaten egg and then coat thoroughly in the panko breadcrumbs. Let the chicken rest for 10 minutes in a cool place, though not the fridge.

In a heavy bottomed frying pan, heat the oil and butter. Let the butter melt, but don't overheat it, as you don't want to burn the breadcrumbs. Lay the chicken carefully into the pan. Let it cook for two minutes, but do make sure that the breadcrumbs are not burning. Turn the chicken over, and cook for another two minutes.

Now transfer the chicken to a roasting dish and baste the top with the liquid from the pan. Place the pan in the middle of the oven and bake for 15-20 minutes. The chicken will be cooked when the cheese melts and becomes gooey. Make sure that the temperature gets to a minimum of 75˚in the centre of the fillets. Let the chicken rest for ten minutes before serving.

Honey Roasted Duck Breast

Duck is my favourite poultry and I love the simplicity of cooking duck breasts. What one finds in most butchers is the breast from the female barbary duck. This happens to be the perfect size for one portion and so is very popular with chefs. However, we produce lovely ducks in Britain, so I would use British if possible.

4 duck breasts

Freshly ground black pepper

2 tbsp sherry

1 tsp chopped curly parsley, to garnish

For the glaze:

1 tbsp runny honey

1 tsp Dijon mustard

1 tsp dark soy sauce

In a bowl large enough to hold one duck breast, mix together the honey, mustard and soy, whisking well to ensure the glaze is well blended. Set aside. Preheat the oven to 180°C.

Pat the duck breasts dry with kitchen paper. Using a sharp knife, score the skin of the duck three times in each direction. Try to cut all the way through the skin, but without cutting into the meat. Season the duck with black pepper, making sure to get it right into the incisions.

Heat a heavy bottomed pan until you see the first smoke. Carefully lay the duck breasts skin side down into the pan. Allow to cook for about 60 seconds. The fat will start to render and will appear in the pan. If the duck is spitting aggressively, turn the heat down a little. After about a minute, remove the duck from the heat. The skin should be golden brown.

Pour any excess fat from the pan and reserve. Using tongs or a fork, run each duck breast through the glaze ensuring that it gets well coated. Place the duck skin side up in an oven pan. Put the pan in the pre heated oven and roast for 15 minutes.

Brush some more of the honey glaze over the breasts. At 15 minutes the duck will be slightly less than 'medium' cooked. If you prefer your duck a little less pink, give it another 5 or 10 minutes in the oven. Remove the duck breasts from the oven and let them rest for 10 minutes in a warm place.

While the duck is resting, remove and reserve any excess fat from the pan. On the top of the stove, over medium heat, add the sherry to the roasting pan to deglaze it stirring in any sediment from the bottom of the pan. Let the sherry reduce by about a half and add the remainder of the honey glaze to the pan. Let it all cook out but don't let it thicken too much. Remove from the heat.

Slice each duck breast across into five pieces. Place each duck breast in the middle of a warm plate. Spoon, or brush, a little of the reduced glaze on each breast, sprinkle with chopped parsley and serve.

It is always worth keeping the fat from duck. It is simply too good to waste. Roast a few potatoes or toss some mushrooms, shallots, cherries or plums in it to accompany your duck breasts.

Serves 4

Roasted Wild Venison with Roast Garlic Sauce

Venison is a meat that was once popular, but then fell out of favour. Like most game, venison is coming back into vogue, and it is a very tasty, healthy option. When ordering venison loin, there is often confusion between the fillet and the loin, further confused by 'tenderloin'. Keep tenderloin out of the conversation. Ask for the 'striploin', not the small fillets. The striploin is as tender as the fillet and is a better size for cooking and portioning. It should be clear of all sinew and fat. Ideally, about 5–6cm in circumference, but this is not critical.

800g wild venison striploin

10 slices pancetta

1 tsp olive oil

For the roast garlic sauce:

2 garlic bulbs

salt and freshly ground pepper

1 tbsp olive oil

½ tsp plain flour

120ml single cream

1 tsp grated Parmesan cheese

Preheat the oven to 180°C.

Slice the tops off the two garlic bulbs, so as to expose the inner flesh. Drizzle well with the olive oil and season with salt and pepper. Wrap the garlic heads in foil, making sure that they are completely encased. Stand in a small ovenproof dish.

Season the venison with salt and pepper and wrap the pancetta around the outside. Rub the joint with olive oil. Now place the loin into your oven pan, making sure that the seams of the pancetta are on the bottom, so they stay in place while cooking.

Place the venison onto the bottom shelf of the oven, and the garlic onto the middle shelf. Roast for 30 minutes before removing them.

Loosely cover the venison loin with foil and allow to rest in a warm place.

Carefully remove the garlic from the foil. When cool enough to handle, squeeze the softened garlic cloves from their papery wrappings into a saucepan. Mix the flour into the garlic and warm gently on the stove for a minute, to allow the flour to cook out. Now add the cream and bring to a simmer. Add the Parmesan and stir well. Let the sauce simmer for another minute.

Aiming at 200g of venison per person. If possible, cut your loin into 8 pieces (allowing 2 pieces per portion) and set them into the middle of warm plates. If you can only cut your venison into 4, that's also fine. Spoon the garlic sauce over the top of each venison serving and serve with your favourite boiled or steamed vegetables.

Roast Grouse with Game Chips and Bread Sauce

Three great British recipes on one plate. If ever British ingredients were to be called into question, here is our answer. Delicious wild grouse with fried potato, bread and milk. Sounds so simple, but, put together, enough to challenge the world. Let's not talk about it, let's get on with it.

The trick to cooking your grouse is to ensure that the meat is just a touch pink where it touches the carcass. If overcooked, the bird will be a little dry. Another thing of note, is that when I first started in the business, the butcher would remove the intestines of the bird ('gut' it) but leave the liver and heart inside. After cooking, the bird would be served to the table with a bread crouton on the side and a small knife, so that the cooked liver and heart could be removed and spread on the crouton, like a pâté'. Sadly, you are very unlikely to come across this today, but you could always ask your butcher for a few game livers to fry off in a pan.

Serves 4

4 medium-sized, young grouse, oven-ready

8 thyme sprigs

4 sage leaves

1 tbsp juniper berries, if the berries are dried, crush them a little

1 tsp olive oil

50g butter

freshly ground pepper

watercress, to serve

Bread Sauce:

10g butter

¼ white onion, finely chopped

250ml fresh milk

¼ white onion, studded with 1 clove

40g white bread, crust removed, bread cut into small pieces

25m double cream

salt and white pepper

Game Chips:

vegetable oil for frying

2 medium-sized Maris Piper or Desiree potatoes, peeled

sea salt

Preheat the oven to 180˚C.

Fill the cavity of each grouse with two sprigs of thyme, one sage leaf and a few juniper berries.

In a heavy bottomed pan, preferably a pan that can be transferred to the oven, heat the olive oil and melt the butter. As the butter starts to foam, put the grouse into the pan breast side down. Allow to seal and colour for 30 seconds. Turn the bird onto the other breast. Don't burn your fingers and control the heat so that the butter doesn't burn either. Allow to cook for another 30 seconds.

Turn the bird onto its back, baste with the cooking juices and give a good twist of black pepper. Put the grouse into the oven and roast for 15 minutes. Remove from the oven and baste well. Loosely cover with foil and leave to stand in a warm place. If you would like your grouse a little more cooked, roast them for 20 minutes.

While the grouse are in the oven, get the bread sauce going. Melt the butter in a saucepan over a low heat and add in the chopped onion. Cook until they are soft and translucent, stirring often, without letting them colour. Pour in the milk. Bring to a simmer and add the cloved onion. Allow to simmer for another 15 minutes. Remove the cloved onion and add the bread. Now simmer gently for 10 minutes. Stir occasionally. Add the cream and season to taste. Turn the heat off but keep warm.

Make the game chips. In a heavy bottomed frying pan, add vegetable oil to a depth of 3–5cm. Heat it so that a small piece of bread will sizzle when dropped in.

Slice the potatoes to 3mm discs. It is best to use a mandolin, or be very careful with your sharpest knife. Pat the potatoes dry with a clean cloth or kitchen paper. Carefully put the potato slices into the hot oil. Remember that it will sizzle, so try not to splash. The potato will cook quite quickly, just 30 seconds to 1 minute. You may need to turn them. When they are golden brown on both sides, remove with a slotted spoon and drain on kitchen paper. Sprinkle with sea salt as soon as they come out of the pan. You will probably need to cook the potato slices a few at a time.

Bring the bread sauce back to a simmer and stir well. Remove the herbs from inside the birds as possible and stand each bird on a warmed plate. Spoon a good helping of bread sauce to one side of the bird and add a few game chips on the other side, with a small bunch of watercress.

Serve to the table with a sauce boat of bread sauce and a bowl full of crispy game chips.

Game

The idea of stalking and catching prey in order to feed the family is as fundamental as food gets. Recent years have seen a decline in the eating of game meat, but to my mind this is an opportunity missed. Game is plentiful and is caught under tight controls via the Environment Agency. Those of us who love it hope to see a renewed enthusiasm for it. From the outside, it would appear that hunting, fishing and shooting has become solely the preserve of the wealthy. However, for country folk these historic ways of catching food are very much a way of life. It is a source of fresh food and the game supply chain is an important source of rural work and income.

There are three main categories of game: furred (animals), feathered (birds) and fish. The hunting of game in Britain is seasonal to protect the animals during their breeding seasons. The start of the season opens with a grand flourish on the Glorious 12th August. Traditionally, dedicated sportsmen head to the grouse moors just before first light on the morning of the 12th, with the sole aim of shooting the first grouse of the new season.

My career has given me a special interest in game. After I had finished my chef's apprenticeship with Roux Restaurants, I took a break from the kitchen and worked for year as a waiter at the Le Gavroche. When it was time to get back to the kitchen, I asked to learn more about meat, as I felt that was a gap in my education. As luck would have it, Chef Albert Roux knew of a top butcher in Paris, and I was soon packed off to Boucherie Lamartine on Avenue Victor Hugo. It was an amazing place and the team there put themselves out to ensure that I learned as much as possible during my six week stay.

When I returned to London, Albert wanted to open a similar shop in Pimlico, and I went to help in the opening process. The shop took the same Boucherie Lamartine name and was a beautiful establishment. Typically, the preparation and presentation of meat took a French style which is why, even today, my shop looks different from other English butchers. Our shop quickly gained a reputation as one of London's top destination butchers. We supplied meat to the Roux group restaurants and many other chefs asked us supply them as well. The wholesale grew to such a level that it was decided to move that part of the business to a butchers shop in Mayfair called John Bailey & Son. This was one of the oldest existing businesses in London specialising in the procurement and supply of poultry and game. The name was changed to Bailey Lamartine and I moved there to run the operation. Quite simply, I fell in love with meat, poultry and game and became destined never to return to the professional kitchen.

The new shop already had a team of skilled and competent 'poultrymen'. The business was churning out thousands of game birds weekly, supplying most of London's top hotels and restaurants, including The Savoy, The Hilton, the Grosvenor House and Inn on the Park. We added our own customer base of restaurants, including Le Gavroche, The Waterside Inn and Le Manoir aux Quat'Saisons. Among the other restaurants we supplied were Pierre Koffman's La Tante Claire, Marco Pierre White's Harveys, Phil Howard's The Square and Simon Hopkinson's Bibendum. It was a rollcall of the capital's best restaurants and their chefs appreciated the quality and expertise we were offering.

One of my proud boasts
is that there are not
many butchers around
who prepare game as
well as I do."

I quickly learnt a lot about the art of preparing game. As with many skills, the process is trickier than it looks. The birds have to be passed through the plucking machine without breaking the skin, then gutted without creating a large, unsightly cavity. The legs must be tied for cooking, without squeezing the breast or cutting the legs. It was tough, time-consuming work. Twelve to fifteen-hour days during the season were not unusual. I had good teachers and I enjoyed learning this new set of skills. One of my proud boasts is that there are not many butchers around who prepare game as well as I do.

The opening day of the game season was always an exciting, adrenalin-packed day. Like many of London's top butchers' shops we would send a van up to Yorkshire to pick up the first birds and race them back to London so they could appear on menus that very night. Back in the shop we would start work at 3am to fulfil orders, then clean the shop and wait for the game birds to arrive. Remember, these were the days before mobile phones so there was no easy way to be in contact with the van – just suspenseful waiting! When the birds did arrive – usually between 5 and 6pm – we raced to pluck, clean tie and dress them. One hundred birds took around an hour to prepare, then off they went in vans to be delivered to the restaurants.

After work we always ended up in the pub to celebrate the start of the season. A very long day, but great fun.

Towards the end of my time at the Roux Restaurants Group, I was asked to do a presentation of game to the chefs and staff at the Grosvenor House hotel, London. It was daunting, but I set about putting together a display of as many different birds and as much furred game as I could get my hands on. On the agreed day, I turned up at the hotel and made a huge display of game in the kitchen. Slowly the chefs started to arrive, then other staff turned up. There were about thirty seats set out, but they were soon filled and there were people standing everywhere. The Head Chef arrived just as I got started and I did my hour. It was nice to get a round of applause and a hearty cheer. I later found out that these sessions were rarely well attended and that thirty chairs were usually optimistic. I received a call from the buying department to thank me for creating so much interest and a very nice letter from the chef thanking me personally.

After the justly revered grouse, partridge and mallard arrive at the beginning of September. There is the red leg partridge, or French partridge, which live and feed in the hedges and spend less time in flight, so becoming plumper and easier to shoot. The grey leg partridge, or English partridge, live in the trees and fly much more. These active birds are a 'dibbing' bird, which means that they dart around the sky in flight, making them much more difficult to shoot. By October the pheasant season starts and the sharp-eyed sportsman are scouring the treetops for the first signs of woodcock and snipe. Pheasants are the most plentiful of the game bird and their abundance makes them affordable. From the sportsman's point of view, the woodcock offers some of the best hunting, with its dibbing flight and small size making it a tricky shot. The snipe

– a much smaller bird – is a close relation of the woodcock. Their rarity make them sought after. The season lasts from August to January, with no shooting allowed on Sundays or Christmas Day.

I am not a fan of hanging game birds for a long time. Certainly, they should be hung for two or three days to allow muscles to relax and sinews to stretch, but tales of leaving birds to hang by the neck until they fall are frankly waffle. The secret of creating a delicious game bird is in the cooking. Undercooked and it will be rare and unappealing. Overcooked and it will dry out. A good butcher covers the breast of every bird with bacon to protect the bird and maintain moisture. The slightest glow of colour on the meat next to the carcass signals a perfect cook. Around 30 minutes in a moderately hot oven (180°C) is a good rule of thumb.

Furred game is also popular in Britain. Venison, hare and rabbit are the main targets, with only venison being eaten in any great quantity in Britain today. The word 'venison' is from the Latin *venari*, meaning to hunt or to pursue. At one time, all game would have been termed venison, as in 'the hunted'. Today, and for many years, Venison has been associated with deer from a number of species. Red deer, Roe, Sika, Fallow and Muntjac, are the more popular in Britain. The season for deer is September to March and is largely regulated by the 'Game Act of 1831', although there have been amendments, including the 'Wildlife and Countryside Act of 1981' which bans the use of 'bows' to hunt deer, or any wildlife for that matter.

Venison is generally considered to have good nutritional values. The wild lifestyle creates healthy, lean meat, largely fat free. Animals feed well on the gorse, heather and natural grasses and herbs of their habitat. The cuts of venison are very similar to beef cuts, offering steaks, roasts, and pieces for pot roasts and stews. Deer breed well and are plentiful, often leading to culling becoming necessary. For some reason, the price does seem to hold at the slightly higher level, which may account for its restricted use, but venison is versatile and delicious, so give it a go.

A bit like offal, game tends to split opinion. Once upon a time, the availability and relatively cheaper prices would have seen much more game being eaten in Britain, but generations have now grown up without game in their diet and are now unfamiliar with how to cook it. It is probably a mistake to discount game completely. I for one would love to see more people discover the joys of eating game.

Roast Duck with Grapes, Thyme and Brandy

Serves 4

A really good wild mallard is something to be cherished. In more recent years, ducks have become more popular with our customers and, certainly at Christmas, they are seen as an upgrade from the humble chicken. While pan frying a breast on its own is a fantastic quick cook in the middle of the week – and the legs make delicious confit – this whole roast duck with red grapes is worth the effort.

1 tsp finely chopped thyme leaves

1 tbsp olive oil

1 tsp balsamic vinegar

sea salt and freshly ground black pepper

1 duck, around 2kg

500g large, seedless red grapes

200ml poultry stock (if you have duck stock, great. If not, chicken stock is fine)

2 tbsp brandy

knob of butter

Preheat the oven to 200˚C.

In a clean bowl, mix the thyme leaves, olive oil and balsamic vinegar. Season the mixture with a little salt and pepper. Pat dry any moisture from the outside of the duck and score the skin about 4 times on each breast. Rub the thyme mix all over the duck, including the inside.

Stand a metal rack in a roasting tin and place the duck on top. Roast in the pre-heated oven for an hour and a half. Baste the duck every 20 minutes or so.

Pour off any excess fat from the roasting tin. Add the grapes to the tin and mix well with the remaining juices. Increase the heat of the oven to 220˚C and return the duck for another 15 minutes

When cooked, remove the duck from the oven into a holding dish. Cover with foil and allow it to rest for at least 15 minutes. When resting poultry, it is a good idea to let it rest on its breast, as this allows the juices to run back through the meat.

Meanwhile, remove the grapes from the oven pan with a slotted spoon and keep to one side. Deglaze the oven dish by adding about a quarter of the stock and scraping all of the goodness from the bottom of the pan. Allow the stock to come to the boil. Sieve the liquid through a fine sieve into a clean pot and add the brandy. Return to the boil and allow to reduce by at least half. Watch out, as the brandy might catch light. If it does, allow the alcohol to burn off but take care. Covering the pot with a well-fitting lid will dampen the flames.

Once the brandy mixture has reduced, add the remaining stock. Once again bring to the boil reducing the sauce until it becomes thick enough to coat the back of a spoon. Bring to the boil and finish by stirring in a knob of butter until it melts.

Portion the duck onto warm plates and garnish with a good helping of the grapes and sauce.

Spatchcock Poussin with Samphire in Sage and Lemon Butter

Serves 4

Some rules are made to be broken, and eating samphire only with fish is one I like to break. I love samphire and this quick and easy, midweek dish bursts with flavour. In principle, 'Spatchcock' means removing the back bone and flattening the bird to aid cooking. Ask the butcher to take out the wishbone first, as it can be sharp.

4 poussin, spatchcocked

Freshly ground black pepper

2 tbsp olive oil

150g samphire*

25g sage and lemon butter
(See p.39)

Cut two incisions, about 4mm deep, on each breast of the poussin. Rub black pepper and the olive oil all over, ensuring it gets inside the incisions.

Heat the oven to 200^{0}C. If you have a cast iron pan that goes from the stove to the oven, that's perfect. If not, never mind, use a frying pan and oven dish. Heat the pan without any oil in it until you see the first sign of smoke. Place the poussin, skin side down into the pan. It will crackle and possibly smoke a little. Leave it to sear for about 30 seconds.

Remove from the heat and turn the birds over. The skin should be crisp and a dark golden brown. Transfer the poussin to the oven and roast for 30 minutes, basting a couple of times with their juices as they cook. At 30 minutes, check that the core temperature of the poussin has got to 75^{0}C, using your meat probe. Remove the poussin from the pan, cover loosely with foil and allow to rest in a warm place.

Return the pan with all its cooking juices to the stove and let it start to sizzle. Throw the samphire into the pan and stir vigorously for about 30 seconds. Add in the sage and lemon butter and continue to stir until the butter melts and just starts to sizzle. Don't let the butter burn. Remove from the stove and adjust the seasoning with black pepper to your own taste.

Place the birds skin side up on a serving dish and spoon the samphire and the juice over the poussin. Serve with a crispy green salad or couscous or indeed both.

There are two things to note here about samphire. Some recipes call for the samphire to be blanched in boiling water, but if you are using fresh, young samphire, the pan cooking is all it will need. The second point that the eagle eyed will have noted that I have avoided adding salt in this recipe. This is because samphire is a coastal plant and already contains enough sea-salt.

Serves 6

Roast Goose with Quince Apple Sauce

A roast goose makes a truly splendid meal. The dark meat has a particular aroma and flavour which is very special. Because of this, I like to cook it simply. An apple and quince sauce is a lovely accompaniment, as it cuts through the richness of the meat. Roasting your own goose also gives you the bonus of an ample amount of goose fat – save it, store it in the fridge and use it to make the best roast potatoes.

1 x 4.5 kg goose, oven-ready (use the neck and giblets to make goose stock to use in gravy)

salt and freshly ground pepper

1 garlic bulb

2–3 rosemary sprigs

Quince apple sauce:

1 good-sized quince, around 350g

juice of ½ lemon

1 Bramley cooking apple

1 cinnamon stick

sugar, to taste

Preheat the oven to 200 °C.

Season the goose well with salt and pepper. Slice the top off the garlic bulb, exposing the cloves inside. Place the garlic bulb and the rosemary inside the cavity.

Place the goose on a rack in a large, deep roasting tin. Cover loosely with foil. Roast for 3 hours. Every half hour spoon off the fat that collects in the roasting tin and reserve (I see roast potatoes in your future…). Remove the foil for the last half hour of roasting and baste the goose with its own fat. Remove the roast goose to a warm serving plate, cover loosely with foil and rest for 30 minutes.

While the goose is roasting, make the quince apple sauce. Peel ,quarter, core and chop the quince into small pieces. Place the pieces in a small, heavy based saucepan mixing them at once with the lemon juice to stop them discolouring. Add in 3 tbsp cold water. Cover, bring the water to the boil and cook covered over medium heat, stirring now and then, until the quince is soft and the water has pretty much cooked off, around 10 minutes.

Peel, quarter, core and chop the cooking apple. Place in a small saucepan with a 1 tbsp water and a cinnamon stick. Cover and cook over a low heat, covered, stirring until softened. Discard the cinnamon stick and mix with a wooden spoon to form an apple purée. Stir in the cooked quince pieces and add sugar to taste. Set aside to cool and serve at room temperature.

Serve the goose with gravy, quince apple sauce, mashed potatoes and red cabbage. A feast.

Serves 4

Chicken Marbella

During the Covid-19 lockdown of 2020, my wife (who runs a cheese shop and restaurant) kept her team together by getting their chef to set a culinary challenge every week. The idea was that they all cooked it and sent each other pictures. Cooking Chicken Marbella was one of the challenges he set, and I couldn't help giving it a go. It's a classic dish, which I understand comes from New York, and is delicious. It can be served with almost anything.

4 chicken legs

80ml white wine

1 tbsp treacle or molasses

For the marinade:

4 garlic cloves, crushed

1 tbsp fresh oregano leaves

2 tbsp red wine vinegar

2 tbsp olive oil

60g pitted green olives, chopped

50g capers, plus a splash of their brine

60g dates, ideally Medjool, pitted

salt and freshly ground black pepper

Score the chicken legs three times and place into a high-sided oven tray. Mix all the marinade ingredients together and pour it all over the chicken, rubbing the chicken legs to make sure that the marinade is absorbed. Cover and marinate in the fridge for not less than 4 hours, though overnight is best.

Preheat the oven to 180°C. Remove the chicken from the fridge and allow it to come towards room temperature. Whisk together the white wine and treacle and pour over the chicken. Make sure to coat the chicken legs well.

Roast the chicken in its oven tray for 45–55minutes, allowing the chicken to brown. Baste it two or three times as it cooks.

Serve the chicken at once, one leg per person, with a generous spoonful or two of the delicious sauce.

BRAISING, STEWING & POACHING

Braising, Stewing and Poaching

Braising

Braising may well be the most underrated of all cooking methods. It has so much going for it. From the finest lamb shanks or the deliciously French Coq au Vin, to the cheaper oxtail or beef shin, braising meat has so much to offer. It can be used to conjure up fine dishes for the smartest tables and is also a great way to cook with cheaper cuts and feed the family on a school night.

Braising combines two methods of cooking. First, the meat is sautéed, or fried, to get some colour into it and start the cooking process – then liquid is added – enough to just cover the meat – and the meat is braised slowly and gently in a covered dish with a tight-fitting lid, usually in the oven. The process is so simple but the permutations of what can be added make for a magical flavour wonderland.

The cooking liquid can very according to budget. For the base, wine or beer is often used, also chopped tomatoes, tomato juice or vinegar. The key being that the acidity in the liquid helps break down the sinews and connective tissues that make up the meat. Usually, stock is used to top up this base, but plain water can be used.

Slow cooking needs time and braising is a method that suits large, fatty cuts of meat, rather than smaller, leaner cuts of meat which would dry out and toughen. A piece of beef brisket, rolled beef shin, a lamb shoulder or shank all lend themselves perfectly to the process. Older and bigger poultry and game birds are ideal for the pot. Cooking on the bone is a real benefit, as the bones release gelatine that boosts the flavour and enriches and thickens the cooking liquid. One tip is to ask the butcher for a bone to add to the pot, then simply remove it when the meat is cooked.

At the end of cooking, the meat should be falling off the bone. Carefully touch the bone and it should wriggle around like a loose tooth, while the meat should be soft enough to break up under pressure from a fork or spoon. Some recipes, such as pulled pork, ask for the meat to be 'shredded' and this can easily be done. Classically, the cooked meat is carefully lifted from the pot and set aside to await serving. The resulting liquid is then slowly sieved into a clean pan and reduced. How much reduction depends on the recipe, but most braised dishes will produce a thick, gelatinous, full-of-flavour sauce, often finished with a knob of butter or a spoonful of double cream for added opulence.

Stewing

Stewing while similar to braising, varies from it in that the meat is totally submerged in the cooking liquid and stews are usually simmered slowly on the stove, rather than cooked in the oven. Stews, by their nature, are served with the cooking liquid. In truth, a good stew is not too far from a hearty soup. Stewing is the ideal way of cooking smaller cuts of meat, such as diced beef chuck or shin, diced lamb neck or shoulder and chicken thighs.

Okay, pay attention, this is important. When buying meat for your stew, make sure your butcher cuts and prepares the pieces so that they are all a similar size and shape. It kills me when I see a butcher offer the requested quantity in higgledy-piggledy sizes. How on earth is the meat supposed to cook evenly?

Where was I? It is a good idea to season and flavour the meat prior to starting the cooking process. For those wanting a thicker sauce at the end, it is often suggested that the meat can be coated in flour at this stage. This is no good if you want to brown the meat and add colour before adding the liquid, as the flour will burn. The other question is whether to put the cooking oil into the pot to heat, or to roll the meat in the oil first. My preference is to toss the meat in seasoned oil first, as I believe that this stops the oil smoking and spitting. Try both and make your own decision. For stews, I like to use a large, heavy-bottomed pot, one big enough to be able to stir the contents around. You need to be able to stir your stew from time to time during the cooking process in order to move the pieces around, so that they cook evenly, and the flavours are shared through the whole stew.

If making a brown stew, the meat should be fried and coloured, then moved to a warm holding dish while the vegetables are browned. The smaller the vegetables are cut, the more surfaces there are to gather up all the goodness from the pan. Once the veg is done, the meat, along with any juices from the holding dish, is added back into the pot. At this point, I would add a thickening agent, and any other ingredients the recipe demands – wine, beer, herbs, spices – before filling the pot with stock or water, adding in herbs or spices and bringing to a simmer on the stove. Now you can relax and open a bottle of wine! If making a white stew using veal, pork or chicken, the process remains the same, but do not allow any colour into the meat or vegetables during the frying stage.

The opportunities for creating a stew are endless. As well as using relatively cheap cuts of meat, other affordable ingredients – vegetables and pulses – can be added for flavour and texture. In my experience, stews taste even better when made a day or so ahead. It's great to cook a stew abundantly, cool it well, refrigerate, and then re-heat on demand for hungry family or visitors. Your stew will last for a maximum of three days if kept in the fridge. Always remember to reheat to above 23^{0}C. There's something very comforting about a hearty stew.

Poaching

A third method of cooking meat in liquid is poaching. Characteristic of poaching is the fact that the liquid simmers very gently indeed, with the cooking liquid often discarded after cooking. It's often used for softer, more fragile cuts of meat, usually poultry, though veal or pork are other options. It is important that the liquid should never boil during poaching, though do remember that cooked meat needs to reach 74°C in its core. Water, stock, wine, beer, milk or a mixture of these are classic poaching liquids. Herbs and spices such as bay leaves, parsley, peppercorns or fennel seeds can be added to the liquid for flavour. It is a healthy way of cooking as requires no additional fat. Meat cooked this way is moist and tender.

WINE ROOM

CCTV IN
OPERATION

BRAISING, STEWING, POACHING: BEEF

Serves 4

Blanquette de Veau

The subtle, lighter, flavour of veal lends itself to this delicate and delicious French stew. It's a classic and will be a hit at any dinner table. As the meat cooks for a good while, there are a number of suitable cuts. I like to use chuck, but the breast would work well. When planning to make your blanquette, it is worth giving your butcher some notice. Not all cuts are readily available, but a good butcher will order it in.

750g veal chuck or breast, diced into 3cm chunks

1 large carrot, peeled and chopped

1 white onion, peeled and chopped

1 celery stalk, chopped

6 white peppercorns

4 cloves

A few sprigs of thyme

Small bunch of curly parsley

salt and white pepper

1 tbsp finely chopped parsley

20 button mushrooms

20 button onions, peeled

30g plain flour

30g butter

125ml double cream

Put the veal chunks in a large pot and cover well with fresh cold water. Bring to the boil, then reduce the heat and simmer for 30 minutes. Skim off any frothy scum that appears on the surface.

After 30 minutes, add the carrot, onion, celery peppercorns and cloves. Tie the thyme and parsley together to form a bouquet garni and add this to the pot. Many people would add a bay leaf to the bouquet garni, but I don't. Do as you see fit. Pour in more fresh, cold water to ensure that the meat is well-submerged, around 4cm above the meat.

Bring back to boiling point, reduce the heat and simmer for a further hour and a half. Continue to spoon off any froth. The contents of the pot must stay covered with water throughout the cooking. If the liquid evaporates, add more water.

While the meat is cooking, ladle off about 500ml of its liquid. In a separate pot, cover the button mushrooms with this liquid and bring to the simmer. Allow to cook for 10 minutes, then remove with a slotted spoon and set aside. Add the button onions to the pot and simmer for 10 minutes or until the onions are soft. Drain the cooking liquid back into the pan with the veal and keep the mushroom and onions together to one side.

After 2 hours, the veal should be tender. Carefully remove it from the liquid with a slotted spoon and keep it warm with the mushrooms and onions.

Sieve the remaining liquid into a clean pot. Discard the vegetables. Bring the liquid in the pot to a boil. Allow it to reduce by about half.

In a small saucepan, make a roux with the flour and butter by melting the butter and mixing in the flour. Now whisk in the veal juice a little at time, so as to avoid lumps, until the roux becomes runny. Now add the roux back into the main pot, to thicken the sauce. Add the double cream. Taste the sauce for seasoning and adjust as necessary. Bring everything to the boil and allow to cook for 5 minutes, before pouring the sauce through a fine sieve.

When it's time to serve, share the warm veal, onions and mushrooms between four bowls and cover with a generous amount of the sauce. Sprinkle with chopped parsley and enjoy.

Pilau rice is a traditional accompaniment and why not? But, just as with any stew, a couple of boiled potatoes on the side would also win the day.

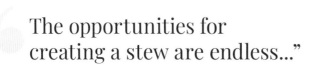

The opportunities for
creating a stew are endless..."

Daube de Boeuf

Serves 4

'Daube' is from the French terracotta cooking vessel, a daubière. I think we are going to have to give this one its full on, French name, Daube de Boeuf. Beef Stew doesn't do it justice. It is a delicious stew from the cheaper cuts, primarily beef. Chuck steak (excellent for burgers by the way), works well here, but shin or flat iron would be good too. Is there anything better than coming in from the cold to a warm house and the smell of a really good stew simmering on the stove?

4 tbsp rapeseed or vegetable oil

150g smoked pancetta, diced

2 tbsp plain flour

Salt and freshly ground pepper

800g lean chuck steak, diced into 4cm cubes

350 ml red wine

2 tbsp tomato purée

1 tbsp Worcestershire sauce

2 tbsp brandy

2 med leeks, white parts only, chopped

1 med white onion, chopped

1 large carrot, chopped

2 celery stalks, chopped

2 garlic cloves, crushed

1 tbsp curly parsley, chopped

250 ml beef stock

For the garnish:

16 baby onions, peeled

16 button mushrooms

Oil and butter for frying

1 tsp chopped curly parsley

In a heavy bottomed pan, large enough to take all of the stew, heat 1 tbsp oil. Sweat off the pancetta, stirring it as you do so, for about 2 minutes, allowing to brown but not to burn. Remove and reserve the pancetta, keeping all of the liquid and residue in the pan.

Add 1 tbsp oil to the pan and heat up over medium heat. Season the flour with salt and pepper and coat the steak in it. Cook the beef in the oil until brown on all sides. You might have to fry the beef in a couple of batches. Remove the beef from the pan and set aside with the pancetta.

Add about half of the red wine to the pan, scraping the bottom to loosen any residue. Let the liquid boil for about one minute. Add the tomato purée, Worcestershire sauce, brandy and the remaining wine. Bring to the boil whilst stirring continuously for two minutes. Remove the pan from the heat and set the pan aside.

In a separate pan, heat 2tbsp oil. Sweat off the leeks, onion, carrot and celery until soft, about 5 minutes. Season well with salt and pepper. Stir in the garlic and parsley for the last minute.

Add the beef, pancetta and vegetables to the reduced wine in original pot. Mix well and bring to the boil. Pour in the beef stock and any residual liquids (for example, the beef may have given off some juices). Cover the pot tightly and simmer on the lowest heat possible for 2 hours, until the beef is tender. Stir from time to time to make sure that the daube is not burning on the bottom.

Uncover the pot and continue to simmer for another hour. Stir well from time to time. The beef should be very soft. Remove the beef and set aside. Strain the liquid into a second, clean pot and bring back to the stove. Discard everything else.

Allow the liquid to reduce to the consistency of a nice sauce. You want it to lightly coat the back of a spoon. Sometimes, getting the sauce to the right consistency, without reducing it away, can be tricky. Chefs use a little trick with flour and butter called a beurre manie. This is basically thickening a sauce with equal parts of flour and softened butter, mixed together, and then whisking the mixture into the boiling sauce bit by bit. Like everything, it takes a little practice, but it's a handy tip. Add the beef back into the pot.

While the sauce is reducing, cook off whichever garnish you want for your daube. Here I am suggesting baby onions and button mushrooms, but any root vegetables would be delicious. Barely cover the onions in fresh, salted water and allow to simmer until soft. Strain and put to one side. Sauté the mushrooms in oil and butter, until cooked, and season well. Put them aside with the onions.

When it's time to eat, put everything together in the large pot, including the garnish, and bring back to the boil, while giving a good stir. Share the daube de boeuf between four deep bowls, ensuring that each dish gets its fair share of the garnish. Sprinkle liberally with chopped parsley and a turn of freshly ground pepper.

Serves 4–6

Chinese Ox Cheek Casserole

Ox cheeks are out of fashion these days, which is a shame as they offer great, tender eating. This Chinese-inspired casserole is very simple to make. It tastes even better if you make it a day ahead then heat it through. Serve with steamed rice or noodles and a green leafy vegetable like bok choy, cabbage or spinach.

2 ox cheeks (1 kg)

2 tbsp groundnut, sunflower or vegetable oil

1 leek, finely sliced

2 spring onions, cut into 2 cm pieces

1 thumb-size piece of ginger, sliced

2 garlic cloves, chopped

4 tbsp dark soy sauce

100ml rice wine/medium sherry

1 litre chicken stock

3 tbsp sugar

1 star anise

½ tsp salt

coriander sprigs, to garnish (optional)

Preheat the oven to 150°C. Bring the ox cheeks to room temperature and pat dry.

Heat the oil in a large casserole dish. Add in the ox cheeks and brown on all sides. Set aside.

Add in the leek, spring onion, ginger and garlic to the casserole dish. Fry for 2 minutes, stirring often, until softened and fragrant.

Return the browned ox cheeks to the casserole. Pour in the soy sauce and turn the ox cheeks coating them in it. Add in the rice wine and cook for 1 minute.

Add in the stock, star anise, sugar and salt. Bring to the simmer. Cover and cook in the oven for 3 hours.

Simmer uncovered on the hob for 30 minutes to reduce the broth down. Garnish with coriander and serve.

Serves 4

Beef Shin a l'Ancienne

Beef shin is bursting with flavour but it takes time to entice the flavour out. This recipe doesn't take long to put together, but there will be plenty of time to do the chores, or pop out for a beer while waiting for it to cook

plain flour, for coating

salt and freshly ground pepper

4 slices of beef shin on the bone (about 200g each, but you will have to work with the butcher on this one. I have never had electric band saws in my shops, so it's all about the skill of the butcher)

2 medium carrots, peeled and halved

2 medium turnips, peeled and quartered

2 celery stalks, halved

12 baby onions, peeled, left whole

4 garlic cloves, peeled

3 sprigs of thyme

1 x 440ml can or bottle of beer (any beer of choice is fine. Stout will give a big, rich flavour or use a good ale)

400ml beef stock

horseradish sauce, to serve

Preheat the oven to 180˚C.

In a large dish or bowl, pour a good helping of flour and season it well with black pepper and salt. Turn each piece of beef in the flour and make sure it is all well covered. Transfer the meat to a large casserole, big enough to hold all of the ingredients.

Turn the carrot, turnip and celery pieces and onions in the remaining seasoned flour and add them to the beef shin, spacing them out. Add in the garlic, thyme, beer and stock.

Bring to the boil on the stove. Cove the casserole tightly. If it has a fitting lid, put one layer of tinfoil across the dish, and then the lid. If there is no lid, two layers of foils should do the trick. The aim is to ensure that no moisture escapes and that the stock doesn't evaporate.

Put the casserole in the middle of the oven and cook for 3 hours. By the end of cooking, the meat will be very tender and falling from the bone. You should be able to pull the beef apart with a fork or spoon.

Serve a piece of the beef into each of four deep bowls. Remove the thyme stalks from the liquid and give everything else a good stir. Adjust the seasoning and share the vegetables and sauce. For those that like it, a good teaspoon of horseradish sauce on top is a delicious final touch. This is a perfect dish to serve with dumplings if you feel so inclined.

MEAT NW5 SHOP
IS HERE TO HELP!
WE HAVE;
ANY CUTS OF MEAT,
CHARCUTERIE & CHEESE
NIBBLES & SCOTCH EGG
FRESH PASTA -PASTA
&
WINE.

Neck Chuck
Rib Eye Rack
Sirloin
Rump
Shoulder
Short Rib
Flank
Silverside & Topside
Point-End Brisket
Shin
Shin

Beef

Buying a piece of decent beef in Britain really shouldn't be difficult. All over Britain we have farmers and farmland capable of producing animals to compete with beef being produced anywhere in the world.

Not so long ago, Aberdeen Angus beef was our benchmark and it is probably still the standard and quality that everything else is measured against today. Hornless Black cattle can be traced to the Highlands of Scotland as far back as the 12th century. By the 1820's, two Aberdeen farmers, William McCombie and Hugh Watson, working independently of each other, had begun the process of producing a breed of cattle noticeable for its quality of meat and ease of rearing. In 1861, Sir George Macpherson-Grant, the 3rd Baronet of Ballindalloch, inherited the estate and took up the challenge of refining the Black Angus breed. The herd that still exists on the Ballindalloch Estate today is descended from the original bloodline. It is the longest surviving bloodline of Aberdeen Angus in the world.

I was very lucky to be offered the opportunity to visit the estate in 1992. It's the type of place that makes you talk a little quieter and be in awe of the greatness that surrounds you. The overriding memory of my visit, apart from the outstanding cattle, was the passion of every single person engaged in rearing cattle on the estate. In 2000, as the millennium New Year's Eve approached, I was fortunate enough to be able to procure two animals from the farm which I sold on the meat counter at Harvey Nichols Foodmarket, Knightsbridge, London. It was an exciting time for the butchers. A small handful of customers – at great expense – got to offer their New Year's Eve guests something that they would be very unlikely to ever come by again. Nearly as rare as the millennium eve itself.

For many years, the Aberdeen Angus brand was almost unbeatable, but farming has changed, customer awareness has changed and farmers, as always, have worked to challenge our perceptions. Today, there are a great many excellent cattle breeds: the huge White Park, the hardy Welsh Black, Belted Galloway, Dexters and the respected Shorthorn are all available. Not every cattle breed offers great meat, but some, including Limousin and Charolais lend themselves to crossing with other breeds to improve muscle structure and eating quality.

When it comes to choosing meat, while breed is a factor, what's more important is the provenance of the beef and the life the animals have lived. Good cattle should be allowed to range free for all of their life. However, in poor weather, animals will be brought in from the fields and kept warm and well fed. It would be mean to leave them in the rain, wind and snow with no shelter and limited food. How would you like it?! When the animals are fed well (as far as possible on natural grass, supplemented with hay and natural sileage) and allowed to exercise, the meat will be full of flavour. Good marbling – the white veining of fat which one sees in beef – is created through good rearing. The best age for a cow at slaughter is a matter of opinion. From about 20 months, a well reared animal will be ready for slaughter. At that age, they will not be big, less than 500kg, but the muscles will be well formed, and the meat will be of a lighter, more subtle flavour. Not so many years ago, older animals would have been frowned upon. However, animals at around 36 months can have fantastic flavour and eating quality.

Fillet

This cut of beef offers the most tender meat. The fillet nestles inside the vertebrae of the animal, running from the rump along the sirloin and is a muscle with no natural bone attachment. Considered the most luxurious of the beef cuts, it commands the highest price. It can be used for grilling steaks or a roast and because of its fat-free nature is best cooked medium or rare. Beef fillet also lends itself to two classic meat dishes: Beef Wellington and Steak Tartare.

Sirloin

The sirloin comes from the saddle area of the animal, sitting between the rump and the fore-rib. In Britain we tend to de-bone the sirloin and cut top quality grilling, or frying, steaks. However, leaving the fillet intact and cutting through the bone, gives you the T-Bone and the Porterhouse steaks. These cuts combine both a sirloin steak and a fillet steak joined by the central 'T' shaped bone and cooked in one piece. Ideally, the Porterhouse should come from the end nearest to the rump, giving a larger fillet eye, and the T-Bone from the end where the fillet tapers away. In practice, however, shops and restaurants rarely differentiate between the two. The sirloin, boned and rolled, is also a prime roasting joint. To my mind, the best cut for a Sunday roast.

Fore-Rib

The fore-rib consists of the four (sometimes five) bones after the sirloin. It is cut square through the bones connecting the rib cage. A good fore-rib is full of gelatinous fats and natural marbling, offering fantastic, 'melt in the mouth' flavours. It is a versatile cut. Similar to the sirloin, it is equally good on or off the bone. For a dinner party show stopper, a standing rib-roast on the bone is always a winner. For the grill or barbecue, the rib can be cut in between the bones to make individual steaks to grill and share. Probably my favourite cut of beef, however, is the rib-eye: the central, round steak in the middle of the rib. Yes, it does make a good roast, but it makes the very best, tastiest beef steak, due to the gelatinous fat running through the middle. Because of this fat and natural juiciness, the rib-eye will suit even those who like their meat well cooked.

Rump

The rump is a hard-working muscle. It sits at the other end of the sirloin from the fore-rib, at the top of the leg. Rump definitely benefits from longer hanging, with a minimum of 25 days being required, but the reward for the time and effort are some very tasty steaks indeed. It is also a very versatile cut, which can be roasted or sliced for a stir-fry.

Topside

The topside is the second muscle at the top of the leg, sitting opposite the rump. It contains very little fat through it, and so doesn't have the versatility of other joints. Despite this, though, the meat is very soft and ideal for roasting rare. This is the perfect joint for rare roast beef'. When sliced, it makes nice minute steaks, perfect for quick grilling.

Silverside

Another of the leg joints, the silverside is so named because of the thick, silver sinew that runs down the side of the muscle when separated from the other muscles. This sinew is strong and tough and is always removed before cooking. The silverside is often prepared as a secondary roasting joint, and can be thinly sliced for minute steaks. It also lends itself to making corned beef or salt beef.

Shin

Before leaving the hind leg, it's worth mentioning the shin. The shin from the hind leg is the better of the two, but the shin from the front leg will not disappoint. If we imagine the work this muscle does carrying the beast, it becomes easier to understand how and why the shin is so full of flavour, producing such wonderful stews and braises.

Oxtail

Right at the back, the tail is made up of a succession of smaller bones that the butcher will separate for you. Each little bone containing meat and natural gelatines offering wonderful flavours for stews and sauces, and, possibly the most famous of all, the oxtail provides one of the world's greatest soups.

Chuck

The chuck, from the forequarter (front) of the animal is a hugely versatile cut. Often known as the chuck 'steak', it most certainly wouldn't be used in the same way as the grilling and frying steaks from the hind of the animal. A dark, chunky meat with good fibres running through, it is ideal for stews and pies, mincing and burgers.

Clod

The clod sits just ahead of the chuck on the shoulder, and towards the neck, and is cut in a similar way. The clod can be fatty and is one of the cheaper cuts. It is not always recognised in a retail shop, but it produces plenty of tasty meat suitable for mincing, making ragu and burgers.

Brisket

From under the neck, the brisket covers the rib cage. The brisket is never going to be a tender joint, but slow cooking in the oven, or more so on the barbecue, gives full of flavour results. Brisket also lends itself to salting, for salt beef. A really good salt beef from the brisket is a triumph created from a very ordinary piece of meat.

Flank

The flank is the belly part of the beast, towards the hind leg. It is just on the edge of being a frying steak, often referred to as the French 'bavette' or skirt steak. Chefs would cut it thinly across the grain and, at most, cook it medium-rare. I always suggest that the flank is a good eating steak, as it will need to be chewed. It is full of flavour and also lends itself to casseroles and stews. It can also be thinly sliced to produce jerky.

Short Ribs

The brisket, chuck, ribs and plate all cover the animals rib cage, and short ribs are just as described They are short cuts across the ribs. Different cultures cut them slightly differently, but in Britain, short ribs are cut parallel to the rib cage, giving about a 15cm-bone, well covered in meat.

Steak and Kidney Pie

For the pastry:
450g plain flour
½ tsp salt
250g chilled butter
iced water

For the filling:
2 tbsp vegetable oil
1 kg chuck steak, diced into
    small chunks
200g diced kidney, diced into
    about 1cm pieces
1 onion, finely diced
1 carrot, finely chopped
40g flour
½ tsp chopped thyme
1 tsp Worcestershire sauce
1 x 330ml tin Guinness
salt and freshly ground black
    pepper
approx. 450ml beef stock

melted butter, for brushing
1 beaten egg, for egg wash

4 x 16cm oblong pie moulds

When I was a young boy, my Dad used to take my sister and I to watch Fulham, at Craven Cottage. I was too young to appreciate some of the great players that we saw, and the historic London football club, but we loved going and we always had a great time. Of course, going out with Dad was always fun. It was exciting going on the buses and tubes and being jostled along by the noisy crowd. We were small and everything else was big. On the colder evenings, as we made our way home, we always hoped that Dad would suggest we had a hot pie, from the man shouting from his van. It made our day. It was steak and kidney. There wasn't a choice, and they were always too hot. We would burn our fingers and, if Dad was hurrying us up, we sometimes burnt our tongue as well, but it didn't matter. We loved those pies.

I'm on the side of the pie makers who believe that a pie has a top and a bottom. Putting the filling into a dish and covering it with a pastry crust, is nothing other than a short cut. Invest in some individual moulds and make good pies. Before lining the mould with pastry, brush it with butter and dust with flour. The pie will cook well and come out clean every time.

Lamb kidneys have a milder flavour than ox kidneys, but both are great for a pie. Try both and choose which you like best. They need to have all of the core removed; this is the butcher's job.

Sieve the flour into a large bowl and the salt. Dice the chilled butter into 2cm cubes and add this to the flour. Rub the butter into the flour with your fingers. Keep rubbing until the mix resembles loose breadcrumbs. Now add a teaspoon of iced water and mix everything together. You want to get to the stage where the pastry comes together in a ball that will clean the side of the bowl. If you need to add a little more water, then do, but the less water added and the less the dough is mixed, the shorter the pastry will be. Once the dough reaches this stage, tip it onto a lightly floured surface and form it into a thick roll. Wrap the pastry in cling film and put into the fridge to rest.

Heat the oil in a large, heavy bottomed casserole dish and fry the chuck steak, stirring often, until browned on all sides. Remove the steak to a holding dish. Add the kidney to the oil and brown as well, then set aside with the steak.

Add the onion and carrot to the pan and fry over a low heat, stirring often, sweating off the vegetables until they start to brown. Now return the steak and kidney to the pan and mix well. Add the flour and mix together well.

Add the thyme, Worcestershire sauce and Guinness to the pan and stir. Season well. Pour in the beef stock, mix well and bring the pot to the boil. Turn the gas down to the lowest setting, cover the pan and simmer for about 1½ hours, until the meat has become soft and tender. If too much liquid cooks off, add a little more stock. When the filling is cooked, set it to one side and allow to become cold.

Prepare the 4 pie moulds by brushing with melted butter and dusting with flour. On a cold surface, roll out the pastry to about 3mm thick. Cut two pastry discs per mould. The first should be 2cm wider than the mould, and the second should be the same size as the mould. Push the first disc into the mould and push down carefully until the pastry is sitting snugly with a little dangling over the edge. Make sure that the pastry is not broken because if so the filling will seep out.

Spoon a portion of the steak and kidney mix into the mould. Don't be tempted to overfill the pie, as this will cause the pie to split during cooking. Brush the edges of the pastry with the egg wash and then lay the second pastry disc over the top. Push down the sides firmly so the top and bottom stick together. Leave to rest for a few minutes before trimming the excess pastry from the sides of the moulds.

While the pastry is still relatively soft, crimp the edges to make a decoration, and pierce a hole in the top to allow steam to escape. You can decorate the pies by rolling out the excess pastry, cutting shapes with your pastry cutters and sticking them to the pie with the egg wash. Rest the pies in the fridge for 30 minutes.

Pre-heat the oven to 200˚.C

Remove the pies from the fridge and egg wash well. The egg wash will make the pies colour and shine beautifully when cooked. Put the pies on a baking sheet and cook in the middle of the oven for 30 minutes until golden-brown.

Ox Tail Ragu

People don't seem to cook with ox tail much these days and that's a shame. Cook it long and slow as in this recipe and you get a lot of flavour from the meat and the bone. This ragu benefits from being made a day in advance and chilled. Serve it with pasta – I like pappardelle – grated Parmesan cheese and a crisp green salad on the side. A glass of red wine would not be amiss either...

25g dried porcini

4 tbsp olive oil

1 kg ox tail pieces

salt and freshly ground pepper

50g pancetta, finely chopped

2 large onions, peeled and finely chopped

1 carrot, peeled and finely chopped

1 celery stalk, finely chopped

2 garlic cloves, chopped

1 bay leaf

300ml red wine

700g passata

700ml water

freshly grated nutmeg

Soak the dried porcini in hot water for 20 minutes. Remove the porcini and chop. Strain and reserve the soaking water.

Heat 2 tbsp olive oil in a large, heavy-based casserole dish over medium heat. Season the ox tail with salt and add in. Fry until lightly brown on all sides. Remove and set aside.

Add in the remaining olive oil and heat through. Add in pancetta, onion, carrot, celery, garlic and bay leaf. Fry, stirring, over medium heat for 5 minutes.

Return the ox tail to the casserole and mix in. Pour in red wine and bring to the boil. Cook uncovered for 8–10 minutes, turning the meat over in the wine, until the wine has nearly all reduced.

Add in the passata, water, porcini and reserved soaking water. Season with salt and pepper. Bring to the boil, reduce the heat to very low and simmer uncovered for 3 hours, stirring now and then.

Remove the ox tail from the ragu and, once it is cool enough to handle, pull the meat off the bones. Return the pulled ox tail meat to the ragu and mix in. Season with nutmeg. Simmer uncovered, stirring often, until heated through.

Serves 4

N16 Meatballs in Tomato Sauce

I think that possibly no two recipes for meatballs are ever the same. I imagine every village in Italy having their own special ingredient. I bet every Italian family has a mother or a nonna who makes the 'best meatballs in the world'. They are truly a comfort food. Easy to make and a great partner for pasta, potatoes or rice, they are well worth the little bit of time and effort. At Meat N16, the guys sell our meatballs as fast as they can make them. Here I have added a simple and delicious, fresh tomato sauce.

Tomato Sauce:

750g Italian plum tomatoes (any tomatoes will do the job, but plum tomatoes are very good)

1 tbsp olive oil

1 large shallot, finely chopped

3 garlic cloves, puréed

1 tsp caster sugar

1 tsp tomato purée

Salt and freshly ground black pepper

Meatballs:

750g pork mince

750g veal mince

2 garlic cloves, crushed

1 tbsp chopped parsley

1 tbsp breadcrumbs

1 tsp fennel seed

125ml red wine

Salt and freshly ground black pepper

2 tbsp olive oil

1 tbsp grated Parmesan

Bring a deep pot full of water to the boil. Take the core out of the tomatoes with the point of a sharp knife and cut a cross in the skin at the bottom. Have a bowl of cold water on stand by. Plunge the tomatoes into the boiling water. Count ten seconds and, with a slotted spoon, remove the tomatoes to the cold water.

Let the tomatoes cool until you can hold them and peel the skin carefully. Sometimes, there might be some soft tomatoes in the salad box. It is tricky to get the skin off of soft tomatoes, but, for a mid-week family supper, a few skins won't kill anyone. Cut the tomatoes in half and discard the seeds. Chop the tomatoes finely or coarsely – as you want them.

Heat the olive oil in a large, heavy bottomed pan over a low heat and sweat off the shallot. Cook for about 5 minutes, stirring, without letting it burn. Add the garlic and sugar and cook out for another 2 minutes. Keep stirring. Finally, add the tomatoes, including any juice, and the tomato purée. Stir well and bring to the boil.

Reduce the heat to the lowest setting and cover the pan loosely with greaseproof paper or a loose lid. Allow to cook for an hour or so, until the sauce has thickened to the consistency of a loose paste. Remove from the stove and keep on one side.

Put all of the meatball ingredients apart from the olive oil and Parmesan into a large bowl. Season well with salt and black pepper. Mix the meatball mix very well, ensuring that everything is blended together.

Divide the mixture into 20 pieces, roll into balls and place on a lightly floured surface, to stop them sticking. I flour my hands as I roll the meatballs, so that they don't stick to my hands.

Heat the olive oil in a heavy bottomed frying pan, add in the meatballs and roll them in the hot oil. Allow the meatballs to cook for 10–15 minutes until they become browned on all sides. Keep the meatballs moving in the pan and adjust the heat as needed to prevent them from burning.

Preheat the oven to 200°C. Once the meatballs are cooked, pour the tomato sauce into the pan and mix the sauce and meatballs together. Transfer everything into a large oven-proof serving dish. Put the dish in the oven for 10 minutes. Remove from the oven and sprinkle generously with Parmesan as you serve to the table.

Lamb

For many reasons – religious, cultural and climatic, lamb is probably the most international and versatile of all meats. It has been a staple part of diets around the world for as long as anyone can remember. Sheep are calm and hardy animals. They thrive in their environment and are easy to care for. Historically, sheep would have been reared on the land and taken to market on foot. Having walked many miles from farm to market, they would be lean and skinny. Their meat would have been tougher and sinewy, but still tasty, and, of course, their woolly coats were a valuable commodity.

Today, in Britain, we produce lamb as good as – if not better than – anybody else in the world.

So, let's quickly mention the Australia question! The Antipodeans produce fantastic lamb. They have the climate and the space. In both Australia and New Zealand much of the economy relies on sheep farming. At Meat London, we get asked all the time why we don't sell Aussie lamb. Quite simply, because British lamb is already fantastic, so why would I want to fly animals all the way around the world? When I go to visit my family in NZ, I won't be searching out British lamb. Wherever you find yourself in the world, eat local!

So, where was I? From Scotland down to the tip of Cornwall, Britain produces top quality lamb. When it comes to Meat London, we dedicate ourselves to lamb from the South and South West. This region, with its lush pastures, gives lambs the opportunity to feed on rich, green grass, producing tender meat which is pink in colour. However, I would agree that the Scots and the Welsh have great lamb, as do farmers in the Lake District and East Anglia. The more hilly or mountainous the region, the stronger the animals will be. Climbing hills means work for the muscles and they become firmer. The flesh is invariably a darker colour. Hillside grasses and natural herbs bring different flavours to the meat. We pay our money, and we make our choice.

By their very nature, sheep are typically free-range, roaming free and living off the grass that grows so well in our damp climate. Through their grazing, sheep take on the characteristics of their locality. This is most evident in sheep from coastal regions that live on salt marshes. Their meat will be a richer colour and carry a pronounced flavour. Their lives are seasonal. Although sheep will lamb from December to May, most lambs are born outside in early spring. In the meat industry and the restaurant world, there is a great buzz of excitement in late spring as the first 'New Season' lambs come onto the market. Lamb, of course, is much in demand for Easter. This pushes the prices sky high for a few weeks, but for those who enjoy the treat, it is usually worth paying for.

At one year, the meat becomes known as hogget. At two years, when the animals have more than two incisor teeth, the meat becomes mutton. This was a meat we used to eat widely in Britain. Nowadays, tastes have changed and it is hard to find retailers selling either as a matter of course. As the lamb ages, the colour of the meat darkens and the flavour becomes that little bit deeper. For me, the best time to eat lamb is just as they are approaching the hogget stage, hogget being the name used for a sheep aged between one and two years. I much prefer the slightly bigger flavours. Today, though, there are not many farmers keeping sheep long enough to become mutton. In the past,

mutton would have arrived naturally, as animals that the farmer couldn't or wouldn't have sold. However, in today's commercial world, the farmers need to get the animals to market and make a profit as soon as possible. Despite the occasional celebrity chef promoting the taste benefits of older lamb, there is not enough interest in mutton to make it commercially viable. We can still get mutton from time to time, and it's always worth asking for if you enjoy flavourful meat. Mutton which has been cooked well is delicious. It has a deep, strong lamb flavour and is especially suitable for slow roasts or stews and braises, where the muscles and sinews have time to break down.

At the other end of the scale from mutton, there is 'milk fed' lamb. Not usually reared in Britain, this is a delicacy in parts of Europe, especially France and Spain. The meat from an un-weaned lamb of 4–6 weeks, typically weighing between 5–8kg, is deemed to be soft and succulent. You are more likely to find it on a restaurant menu than in the local high street butchers.

When buying lamb, look for the meat to be a deep pink, not quite purple in colour.

The eye of the meat should be clear of any imperfections. Lamb, like beef, does have marbling running through it, but it's not visible in the way that beef marbling is. There should be a crisp white fat covering of no more than 2–3mm. The best butcher's shops will remove the skin from most cuts, since it can be very tough. It's a simple task for the butcher which adds to the enjoyment of eating lamb.

In the butchery world, we split the lamb, or 'break it down', into four primal parts: legs, saddle or loin, shoulders and best-end or racks. In the world of meat – and despite animals walking on all fours – they always only have two legs, and the front 'legs' are always referred to as 'shoulders'. No, I don't know why. We also get the breast, which is quite fatty but, if prepared well, offers a delicious, cheaper, slow roast. The other significant cut is the neck chops, for which see my Chops essay (p.44). Because of its soft, tender nature, lamb is a very versatile meat that lends itself to a number of cooking methods. The same succulent leg that we roast whole for Sunday lunch, eats just as well if butterflied for the barbecue or cut into steaks for the grill.

Leg of Lamb

A popular cut for a traditional roast, a whole leg of lamb weighs 2kg–3kg and will feed over six people. It is a great showpiece for a Sunday lunch. One of my favourite things to do, is to 'tunnel bone' the leg and tie it with twine so that the meat retains the shape of the leg. This makes it so easy to carve and cuts out any wastage. On the other hand, if you are fewer than six, then your butcher should happily cut the leg up for you. The leg has three sections: the shank (shin), the middle and the rump or chump.

Saddle of Lamb

Another classic cut for a roast, I have to admit that this is my favourite cut of lamb. It's my absolute 'go to' cut for a dinner party. When boned and rolled properly, the saddle has everything you need. It is a very meaty cut, it has the tenderness of the two 'eyes' (fillets) from the middle of the animal and it's attractive and easy to serve. Have the butcher de-bone and roll the whole saddle, minus the rump. The piece will weigh between 1kg and 1.5kg and is perfect for 6–8 people. Boned and rolled, the piece should be a virtually perfect cylinder shape, thus ensuring that the joint can be cooked to the same degree all the way through. To serve, cut it into slices about 2cm thick. It's not necessary to carve the saddle at the table. The beautiful, disc-shaped pieces give your inner chef the chance to shine and present it nicely. For those who like stuffing, the saddle's shape makes it perfect to get a nice even filling throughout.

Cannon of Lamb

A banquet chef's delight. The cannon is one half of the saddle, in which the eye (fillet) is removed from the saddle. All the fat and sinew is cut off, leaving just pure meat. It is very tender and undoubtedly delicious, typically weighing around 350g. However, it is outrageously expensive. A great treat.

Rack of Lamb

I've never been quite sure why a little two, or three, bone rack of lamb gets banqueting chefs so excited. How many times have I sat at a smart dinner and struggled to get the meat off the bone with my knife and fork? However, roasting a rack for a small gathering is a nice thing to do. The rack is the first eight bones of the ribs, after the saddle. We take the best end of the lamb and split it through the vertebrae or chine bone, to get two racks. Two bones are enough for a portion with a good accompaniment (a large, unctuous chunk of Gratin Dauphinoise always does it for me, see p.276). The meat from the rack is soft and juicy, and there will be little fat. Invariably, nowadays, the rack will be prepared 'French Trimmed'. This means that the butcher will have cleaned about a third of the bone to the top of the rack. This practice divides opinion. Some people regard trimming the top section a waste of meat. I like to see it trimmed, providing not too much bone is exposed. It's attractive and gives something to hold while nibbling the cutlet. A good butcher will 'chine' your rack for you. This is sawing through the vertebrae bone, since you would not be able to cut through it once cooked. The butcher should then neatly tie the bone back in place so that you can roast your rack standing on its base, with the bone making a natural trivet. Once cooked, snip the twine and you will be able to portion your rack accordingly.

Shoulder of Lamb

This is absolutely the best joint for slow roasting. The shoulder is fattier than other cuts and a little more sinew-y. It takes longer to break down in the cooking process, and benefits from long, gentle cooking. Gently warm your oven at around 150 ˚C. Put the shoulder on a rack in a roasting tin into the oven, close the door and open the wine. The important thing when slow roasting is to baste the meat regularly after the first hour. If the meat starts to over colour, then a loose fitting, tin foil cover will do the trick. Don't be tempted to seal the edges of the cover as this will cause the meat to poach. You will know when the meat is cooked, as the bone will pull away easily when given a little tug (try not to burn your fingers!). An average whole shoulder weighs 2kg – 2.5kg on the bone and would easily serve between 6–8 people. For a smaller gathering, ask the butcher for a half shoulder. The shoulder also lends itself to being boned and rolled.

Rump of Lamb

During the 1990s, every stylish, new restaurant seemed to offer rib eye steak and quasi d'agneau (lamb rump) on its menu. Despite the enthusiasm shown by chefs, this cut has never sold well in retail. I think this is the butcher's fault. It's a fantastic cut and perfect for two people and could feed three at a push. The rump is the small, triangular, boneless cushion at the top of the leg. I get a little buzz every time a customer asks me for a slightly smaller leg because I know I'm about to create another great joint just by cutting off the rump. Two happy customers with one cut!

Apart from a thin covering on the outside, it is pretty much fat-free. It makes a perfect mid-week roast or is just as good for Sunday lunch. Heat a solid bottom pan. Score the surface of the rump and season with herbs or spices. Place the rump into the hot pan fat side down. Within thirty seconds, the fat will start to melt and spit a little. Turn the rump over and straight into the oven preheated to 190 ˚C. It will take about 30 minutes for medium. Ample time to blanch some green beans and toss them in melted butter.

Middle-Neck of Lamb

At the end of the best-end of the lamb, there are four bones before the neck starts. We call this the middle-neck. We can cut this into lamb chops, which are perfect for the barbecue or lamb stews. They are termed a 'secondary' chop, but they are full of flavour. This is also the start of the lamb neck fillet.

Neck of Lamb

The neck is about 10–12cm long, and the bone itself is covered with a good layer of meat. By cutting through the neck at around 3cm intervals, we get a sizeable chop ideal for braising – see Lancashire Hotpot (p.234). The meat around the neck can be removed to produce a fillet.

Neck Fillet of Lamb

By removing the fillet from both the middle-neck and the neck in one go, we forgo the chops, but we gain a lovely piece of meat. The neck fillet is not as pure as the meat from the saddle or the rack but it has all of the flavour. It can be grilled or barbecued or diced up to use in stews, braised dishes or curries (see Lamb Curry p.237). It can also be used to make skewers for the barbecue.

Breast of Lamb

The final cut from our lamb, is the breast, traditionally a cheap cut. The breast is quite versatile, but it will always be fatty, and will need to be prepared carefully. It is best to remove as much fat as possible before cooking. The breast can be marinated on the bone and slow cooked, as a lamb 'spare rib'. It can also be de-boned, seasoned with herbs and spices, and rolled tightly to slow roast for 2–3 hours. Depending on how many people to be fed, two or three breasts could be laid on top of each other, rolled and tied tightly before cooking. Cooked with care, the breast can be very delicious indeed.

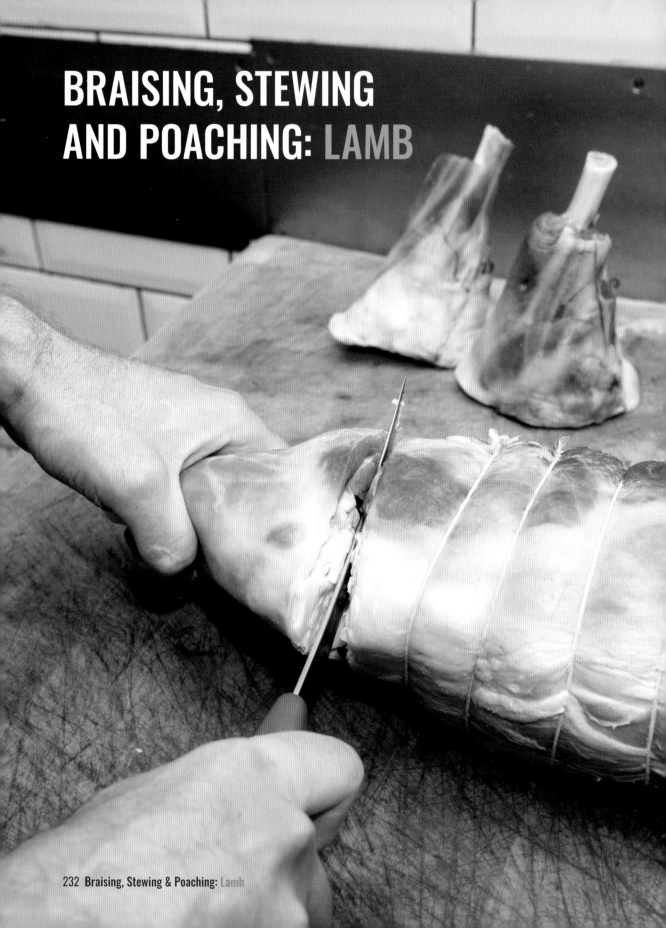

BRAISING, STEWING AND POACHING: LAMB

Serves 4

Braised Lamb Shanks

The lamb shank always looks so big, but it cooks down to a perfect portion every time. It is important to get the shank from the back leg. They are more meaty and they will cook better. Don't be conned into believing that the front 'leg' will do the same job. It won't, as the bone to meat ratio isn't right. The recipe calls for the stock to be sieved, but, on a cold night, when it's just two of us for dinner, I am happy to add the vegetables that braised with the lamb, back into the sauce. Delicious.

4 tbsp vegetable oil

4 lamb shanks, each around 300g

1 large onion, chopped

1 large carrot, chopped

1 large celery stalk, chopped

3 garlic cloves, chopped

1 tsp tomato purée

2 tsp Worcestershire sauce

1 tbsp plain flour

250ml red wine

750ml brown stock (see p.266)

1 bouquet garni (sprigs of thyme, rosemary, parsley, sage tied up with string)

Flat leafed parsley, to garnish

Preheat the oven to 180°C.

Heat 2 tbsp oil in a heavy bottomed casserole dish. Add in the lamb shanks and fry, turning as required, until they are browned all over. When well coloured, remove from the casserole and keep to one side.

Heat the remainder of the oil in the casserole. Add in the onion, carrot and celery and cook off. Cook, stirring now and then, until they take on some good colour. Add in the garlic, tomato purée and Worcestershire sauce. Mix well for about a minute. Add in the flour and mix well.

Pour the red wine into the casserole. Bring to the simmer and allow the wine to reduce for 5 minutes. Return the lamb shanks to the casserole, together with the stock and bouquet garni. Stir the pot to mix everything together. Bring the stock to a boil. Cover with a lid and cook in the oven for 1½ hours.

At this stage, the lamb will be soft and falling from the bone. Carefully remove the shanks to a warm holding dish and loosely cover with foil. Bring the casserole dish back to the stove and, giving it a good stir, bring the liquid to the boil and reduce to a thick sauce that easily coats the back of a spoon. Sieve the hot liquid into a clean pot, discarding everything else.

I only ever eat lamb shanks with mashed potato but be as adventurous as you like. Place a good spoonful of mash in the middle of a deep plate and stand a hot lamb shank on top. Spoon a very generous helping of the sauce over the top and sprinkle with a little flat leaf parsley for colour.

Lancashire Hotpot

Serves 4

A proper working class dish that conjures up the feel-good factor and a thick Lancashire accent. The flavour of the lamb neck combined with the soft, oven-singed potatoes is pretty heady stuff.

8 lamb neck chops, 2cm thick (don't get fobbed off with middle-neck chops)
100g butter
1 tbsp vegetable oil
3 lamb kidneys, cored and each cut into 6 pieces
1 large onion, sliced
1 medium carrot, peeled and chopped
1 celery stalk, chopped
Salt and freshly ground pepper
2 tsp plain flour
3 tbsp Worcestershire sauce
500ml lamb or beef stock
1 bouquet garni*
1 kg potatoes, peeled, cut into ½cm thick slices – Maris Piper or Desiree will do the job

Preheat the oven to 180°C. If the butcher has been lazy, trim any excess fat from the neck chops. Melt 50g butter in a thick bottomed pan and add a spoonful of oil. The oil will help to stop the butter burning. As the butter starts to foam, brown the lamb chops on both sides before removing them to a deep casserole. Add the kidneys to the butter, fry until browned on all sides and remove to the casserole dish with the lamb.

Add the onion to the pan and stir well. Add a little more butter if needed. Add the carrot and celery and continue cooking until they are all starting to brown. Season well with salt and black pepper. Tip the flour into the vegetables and mix well. Add in the Worcestershire Sauce and brown stock and stir or whisk vigorously until everything combines into a beautiful sauce. Pour the sauce over the lamb and kidneys in the casserole. Add the bouquet garni.

Now is the time to get creative. Layer the potato slices over the meat, working your way around the casserole dish and overlapping the slices as you go and making sure that the circles overlap each other. Keep going until you have created a 'cover' of potato slices. Melt the remaining butter and brush the potatoes before covering the casserole with a loose lid, or aluminium foil. Cook in the oven for about 1½ hours.

Remove the casserole from the oven, take off the cover and butter the potatoes again. Return the casserole back into the oven for 15–20 minutes. The potatoes should be coming towards a golden brown. If necessary, two minutes under the grill will finish them off.

To serve, dig through the potato and share the lamb and kidneys between 4 bowls, or deep plates. Ladle in some of the juices from the pot and finally share out the potato. Watch the smiling faces.

A bouquet garni is a way of imparting some lovely herb flavours into your stew without leaving the herbs inside. Thyme, rosemary, sage, parsley etc can all be bundled up with string and dropped into the pot. Always remember to take it out again at the end. By the way when I was a young apprentice, Chef Albert Roux would never use bay leaf, as he said it was bad for the heart. I have never used bay leaf.

Serves 4

Lamb Pistachio Korma

This is a very classy curry indeed. Fragrant spices, pistachio nuts and double cream combine to make it a real treat. The braising time for the meat is under half an hour, so I recommend using tender lamb neck fillet which works very well here.

4 tbsp oil

2 large onions, peeled and finely chopped

4 garlic cloves, peeled and chopped

2.5cm root ginger, peeled and finely chopped

2 cinnamon sticks

10 green cardamom pods

3 tsp ground coriander

½ tsp chilli powder

800g lamb neck fillet, diced into 2.5cm pieces

100g pistachios, finely ground

200ml hot water

salt and pepper

150ml double cream

1 tsp garam masala

1 tbsp chopped pistachios, to garnish

small handful of coriander leaves, to garnish

Heat the oil in a deep, heavy-based, lidded pan. Add in the onion and fry for 20 minutes over medium low heat, stirring often. Add in the garlic, ginger, cinnamon and cardamom and fry for a minute, stirring.

Mix the ground coriander and chilli powder with 1 tbsp water. Add this to the onion mixture, mixing in, and fry, stirring, for a further minute.

Add in the lamb and mix, coating well with the onion mixture. Mix the ground pistachios with a little of the hot water to form a paste and mix this in with the lamb. Add in the remaining hot water. Season with salt and pepper.

Bring to the boil. Cover and cook over medium heat for 20 minutes, stirring now and then. Uncover and, stirring as you do so, gradually mix in the double cream and garam masala. Simmer gently over a low heat for 5 minutes, stirring often.

Garnish with pistachios and coriander leaves and serve at once. Basmati rice goes beautifully with this.

Yavini's Durban Lamb Curry

Serves 4–6

Richard, my business partner, and his wife, Yavini, have two delightful daughters and they have all supported the business from the get go. Now Yavini wants to add her own touch to our book and is sharing a family recipe. 'Home to a fascinating mix of cultures, Durban swelters on the Indian Ocean coast of South Africa. This knockout recipe has been passed down the generations of my family that hailed from South India'.

5 medium potatoes, Maris Piper works well

1 thumb size piece fresh ginger, peeled

4 garlic cloves, peeled

2 tbsp sunflower oil

2 tsp fennel seeds

2 cloves

2 cinnamon sticks

1 kg of lamb diced, leg or shoulder, we like the meat lean

2 large onions, chopped

1 x 400g tin of good-quality chopped tomatoes

1½ tsp salt

Fresh curry leaves

1 tsp garam masala powder

Fresh chopped coriander, to garnish

For the masala mixture:

2 tsp coriander powder or, even better, freshly ground from seed

2 tsp cumin powder or, even better, freshly ground from seed

2 tsp chilli powder, adding a bit more if you want a 'spicier' curry

Dice the potatoes and par-boil them in boiling water for 5 minutes. Drain and set-aside

Pound the ginger and garlic together into a paste. Make the masala mixture.

Heat the sunflower oil over a medium heat in a deep, heavy-based pot. When the oil is hot add in the fennel seeds, cloves and cinnamon sticks, allowing the fennel seeds to pop but not to burn.

Add the diced onion and cook for a few minutes on the same medium heat until soft, not caramelised. Mix in the ginger and garlic paste and fry for another minute until fragrant. Stir in the masala mixture, then add the diced lamb with the salt, mixing to coat it with the flavourings.

Cover the pot and start to cook gently on a low heat for 15 minutes, stirring occasionally to ensure the lamb doesn't stick and adding a little water if needed to stop it burning. Stir in the canned tomatoes, cover and simmer.

After 30 minutes add the par-boiled potatoes, a few curry leaves and around 125ml water and mix in.

After another 10 minutes of simmering – when the lamb is tender to taste and the potatoes are cooked but not overcooked – remove the curry from the heat

As the curry cools, sprinkle the garam masala and fresh chopped coriander over the top of the curry.

Serve the curry with basmati rice and or your favourite bread, a side of dhal and a cooling cucumber yoghurt raita or yoghurt and mango pickle.

BRAISING, STEWING AND POACHING:
PORK

Meat London Smoked Cassoulet

We have a small, cold smoking shed in the garden at Meat N16. A few years back, the boys were driving me mad to buy it. For a long time, I was reluctant; the guys often come up with a thousand reasons why I should buy another piece of equipment and then it never gets used. Anyway, I succumbed and to their credit, they have produced our popular 'Middle Cut, Meat London Bacon' over the years, which our customers love. More recently, a new guy, Sal, joined the Team and he has started smoking Toulouse sausages and pork necks. They are to die for, so, rather than offer the tried and trusted, classic cassoulet recipe, here is my own version, proudly showcasing items from our very own smoker.

2 tbsp olive oil

Freshly ground black pepper

4 Meat London smoked Toulouse sausages

2 red peppers, cut into 4 pieces lengthways

2 yellow peppers, cut into 4 pieces lengthways

8 banana shallots, peeled

30g butter

1 tbsp sugar

4 x1cm thick slices Meat London smoked pork neck

1 x 700g jar white haricot beans or chickpeas, drained

1 x 400g tin chopped tomato

1 tbsp curly parsley, chopped

Preheat the oven to 180˚C.

Pour the olive oil into a large oven dish and season it with black pepper. Add the smoked Toulouse sausages and the pepper pieces and mix everything in the oil. Roast on the middle shelf of the oven for 30 minutes.

At the same time, put the shallots into a pot and add just enough cold water to cover the shallots. Add the butter and sugar and simmer until the liquid evaporates and the shallots are softened and glazed.

Using either a griddle or a heavy bottomed pan, cook the smoked pork neck for one minute on each side.

Once the Toulouse sausages have cooked for 30 minutes, add the shallots and pork neck to the oven dish and turn off the oven, leaving the dish inside.

In a large casserole, mix together beans and tomatoes. Use the tomato tin to add one tin full of cold water. Bring to the boil and allow to simmer for five minutes. Season to taste with black pepper. The smoked meats and tinned tomatoes will bring enough salt.

Remove the dish from the oven and carefully cut each sausage in half across the middle, on an angle for aesthetics. Finely slice the peppers, mixing the colours together.

Spoon a good helping of the beans into 4 deep dishes. Top each serving with the sausages, shallots and pork neck. Add the sliced peppers on top and finish off with a sprinkling of chopped parsley. Get the dishes to the table while still piping hot.

....

If the smoked Toulouse are not available, the French saucisse de Morteau are a delicious alternative, as is the Polish kielbasa. Similarly, a good pancetta could replace the smoked pork neck.

If you prefer to cook your own beans, the night before you want to make the cassoulet, put 400g of dried haricot beans into a bowl and cover with three times the volume of cold water for the volume of beans. Let them soak overnight in the fridge. When it's time to cook the beans strain them and pour them into a large pot. Add three measure of water for every measure of beans and salt well. Allow them to simmer, loosely covered, for between 1 and 1½ hours until they are softened but retain texture. Strain well and use in the recipe.

Braised Kimchi Meatballs

Meatballs are such versatile things. You can experiment with different meats – beef, lamb, pork, chicken – and mixtures of meats. Then, of course, there are the flavourings you add to the mince – so many herbs and spices to play with. Korean kimchi adds a nice little kick of chilli to these tasty pork meatballs. Serve with steamed rice and leafy greens – savoy cabbage or bok choi – for a satisfying meal.

For the meatballs:

500g pork mince

2.5cm root ginger, peeled and grated or finely chopped

100g kimchi, finely chopped

½ tsp salt

½ tsp sugar

1 egg, beaten

2 tbsp cornflour

1 tbsp sesame oil

1½ tbsp oil

1 onion, peeled, quartered and sliced

1 garlic clove, peeled and chopped

1 red pepper, cut into short strips

140g tin of pineapple chunks

a splash of dry sherry (optional)

1 tsp tomato purée

200ml chicken stock

salt and freshly ground pepper

Mix together all the meatball ingredients thoroughly. Shape into ping-pong ball-sized meatballs and chill in the fridge for 20–30 minutes to firm them up.

Heat 1 tbsp oil in large, lidded, non-stick frying pan over medium heat. Add in the meatballs – frying them in 2 batches – and fry until lightly browned on all sides. Be sure to turn them gently! Remove and reserve.

Ad the remaining oil to the pan and heat through over medium heat. Add in onion, garlic and red pepper and fry, stirring often, until softened. Add in the pineapple chunks and fry for 2–3 minutes until lightly coloured on both sides.

Return the meatballs to the pan, mixing them well. Add in a splash of sherry and allow it to sizzle briefly. Mix in the tomato purée and pour in the stock. Season with salt and pepper.

Bring to the boil, cover partly, reduce heat and simmer for 20 minutes, turning the meatballs now and then to ensure they cook evenly.

Poultry

A chicken roasting in the oven takes over the whole house in the best possible way. On a cold winter's day, opening the front door to the smell of roast chicken immediately lifts the spirits. On heady, hot summer days, the scent of the chicken is a tantalising fragrance. What child hasn't hung around the kitchen, coveting a little piece of crisp skin, or a juicy wing from the bird just out of the oven? And when the meal is over and we fall back into our seat, replete and happy, the bird's carcase can be transformed into a comforting bowl of soup to enjoy the day after.

British people are sometimes quite staid in their approach to poultry. We love our roast chicken but seem to be nervous at the thought of cooking a duck or a guinea fowl. My advice, is take a deep breath and get over it. We have some amazing poultry in this country, and it seems a shame to restrict ourselves.

It's important to start at the beginning. Don't imagine that a chicken is a cheap product. It takes time to grow a chicken properly. They need to get fresh air and roam around. They need to eat well and have plenty of space. Ask your butcher where the birds come from? Do they have the opportunity to roam free? Are they well fed. Birds need to grow slowly and naturally ,developing their bones, muscles and flavour.

Poultry is a truly versatile meat, which is why it is so popular. All birds – chickens, turkeys, ducks, geese, guinea fowls, poussin and game birds – can be prepared and cooked in the same way.

Trussed or not?
As is often the case, there are different schools of thought! My own preference is to put herbs and seasoning or stuffing inside of the bird's cavity and truss it up. It keeps the bird in shape during cooking and, in my opinion, helps ensure even cooking throughout. The second school of thought is that if the bird is not trussed, the hot air can get inside and assist the cooking. I suggest you do whichever you prefer.

Supreme and Fillet
In poultry butchery, the word 'supreme' comes from the French. It signifies the breast being removed from the carcase with the skin left on and the first joint of the wing intact. This is a cut that chefs are fond of. The crisp, golden skin would form part of the visual appeal. The fillet is the same breast, but minus the skin and wing. If you want the breast with the skin on, just ask your butcher to cut the wing off. Which cut you're going for depends on your cooking method. If you are going to grill, roast or barbecue it, then it is best to keep the skin on as this protects the flesh from the direct heat and helps keep it moist. If the poultry is to be cut up for stir fry, stews or curries or to be flattened and breadcrumbed, then best to have the skin removed.

Leg
The leg comes either whole or cut into its two component joints. By cutting the leg through the middle joint, we create the drumstick and the 'high. From medium sized birds – such as chickens, guinea fowls and ducks – the drumstick is great for finger food. The thigh is meatier, making it ideal for barbecuing, grilling or roasting. The leg is more robust

than the breast – with the meat darker and full of flavour – and takes a longer cooking process. A whole leg can be roasted or grilled and is ideal for rubbing with herbs and spices or marinating. A classic French way of treating duck or goose legs is to confit them, that is gently poaching them in fat, until the meat is ready to fall from the bone. The confited leg is then finished under a hot grill to crisp the skin.

Wings

Wings are finger food, perfect for parties, buffets and picnics. Depending on the size of the bird, or the desired portion size, your butcher should be able to give you a two or three joint wing. Wings are fantastic dry-rubbed or marinaded, then cooked slowly in the oven or on the barbecue. Don't be afraid to get your face all messy; some things are just meant to be!

Carcase

The carcase is often an overlooked asset. In Taking Stock (p.264), I explain how to turn your poultry carcase into tasty stock which can then be used for soup, stews or sauces.

Spatchcock

In principle, the art of spatchcocking a bird is that of removing the vertebrae and flattening it. This allows rubs and marinades to penetrate more of the bird and to get more direct heat to the bird, so reducing cooking time. One can oven roast a spatchcock, but they are much better on the barbecue or grill. However, there are a couple of things to ask your butcher to do. Firstly, always get the wishbone removed. Secondly, make sure that the breast of the bird is well scored, as this helps the flesh absorb rubs and marinades, making for tastier results.

BRAISING, STEWING AND POACHING:
POULTRY AND GAME

Thai Green Chicken Curry

2 tbsp oil

1 portion of green curry paste (see below)

600g boneless, skinless chicken thighs, chopped into small chunks

1 x 400ml tin coconut milk

2 x 225g bamboo shoot slices, drained

dash of fish sauce

1 tsp sugar

6–8 Thai lime leaves

1 red chilli

handful of fresh Thai basil leaves/basil leaves

For the green curry paste:

2 lemongrass stalks

Thumb-size piece of galangal or fresh ginger, peeled and roughly chopped

1 tsp cumin seeds

1 tsp coriander seeds

1 tsp peppercorns

1 nutmeg

4 cloves

2 shallots, peeled

3 garlic cloves, peeled

4–6 small green chillies, stems trimmed – de-seed the chillies if you want to reduce the heat

1 tsp Thai shrimp paste

50g fresh coriander, including roots and stalks, roughly chopped

grated zest of 1 lime

1 tsp salt

This is such a much-loved Thai dish for a reason. Yes, you can buy readymade Thai curry pastes. Yes, you do have to track down some ingredients for the paste, but when you make this Thai green chicken curry yourself from scratch it really does taste rather special.

First, make the green curry paste. Peel and discard the tough outer casing from the lemongrass stalks. Chop the lower white bulbous part of the stalks, discarding the fibrous remainder.

Place the lemongrass and all the other curry paste ingredients in a food processor. Blitz together to form a thick paste.

Heat the oil in casserole dish or heavy based pot over a low heat. Add in the green curry paste and fry, stirring often, for 5 minutes until fragrant. Add in the chicken pieces and mix to coat with the paste.

Pour in the coconut milk, mixing well. Add in the bamboo shoots, fish sauce, sugar, lime leaves and whole red chilli. Stirring, bring to the boil. Reduce the heat and simmer for 20–25 minutes until the chicken is cooked. Garnish with basil leaves and serve at once. Jasmine rice is the perfect accompaniment.

Pot-Roast Cock Pheasant with Chestnuts and Pancetta

Serves 2

I only suggest a cock pheasant because they're usually a little larger and give two good portions. A large hen, or even two smaller hens, will serve just as well. The game season runs through the colder months, and this is another potful of winter cheer to come home to. Now here's a thing; I'm not much of a real ale drinker, but I can see myself enjoying a small glass of porter with this.

1 cock pheasant, gutted and trussed

2 tbsp sunflower or vegetable oil

Salt and freshly ground pepper

½ red onion, roughly chopped

1 large carrot, roughly chopped

2 celery stalks, roughly chopped

1 garlic clove, chopped

1 small bunch of fresh thyme

2 tsp plain flour

200ml sweet sherry

½ litre chicken stock

50g diced pancetta

100g cooked, peeled chestnuts

Preheat the oven to 190°C.

Your butcher should have gutted the pheasant and it should be trussed ready for the oven. Rub it all over with 1 tbsp oil and season with salt and pepper. Heat a heavy bottomed casserole and carefully brown the bird all over. Mind your fingers. Remove the bird to a dish and keep to one side.

Heat the same casserole and add in the remaining oil. Add the onion, carrot and celery and stir until they start to colour. Add the garlic and thyme and cook for a minute. Mix the flour in, which will make the mix become pasty, and stir for 30 seconds. Now add the sherry. Mix in, scraping the bottom of the pot to loosen any tasty sediment. Pour in the stock, mixing in well, and bring to a simmer.

Carefully put the pheasant back into the liquid and cover the casserole with a tight fitting lid or foil. Place the casserole in the oven and cook for 1 hour. When the bird is cooked, the bone will come away from the leg with a light tug, or, if you prefer, use your probe thermometer to confirm that the bird has reached 75°C inside. Carefully take the pheasant out of the liquid and rest it in a warm place, loosely covered.

In a separate, heated saucepan, toss the diced pancetta until it cooks through, gives off some oil and starts to colour. Pour off any excess oil and stir in the chestnuts. Remove from the heat and strain the cooking liquids from the casserole through a fine sieve into the saucepan. It's possible to adjust the consistency of the sauce by adding a little stock if it is too dry or reducing if it is too loose. Season to taste and set to one side.

When ready to serve, remove the legs and breasts from the pheasant and put them in the middle of a two warm plates. Bring the sauce back to a simmer and spoon a good helping over the pheasant, ensuring that each portion gets some chestnuts and pancetta. Serve immediately with a sauce-boat of the remaining sauce on the side.

the Sausage

the Lamb

the Steak

the Bird

info. ask member of Staff

Paul Grout,
Meat London

Paul first served me at Boucherie Lamartine in 1984, I had never spent
so much on a few sausages. He is a butcher through and through
and every conversation about meat over the years has been a 'school
day' and I have come away with just a little more knowledge and
understanding every time. It is his love of craft, skill and good meat
that shines through.

Long before it became the norm to have a close and detailed working
relationship with your wholesale butcher, as a chef, Paul would share
his knowledge of the lesser great cuts of an animal, his time as a chef
meant he talked to chefs and 'cuts' with an understanding of what they
wanted to achieve. Araignée steaks, andouillette from Bobosse in Lyon,
rumps of veal and new seasons lamb's kidney encased in their fat that
were as delicate as poached eggs, these were all introduced to me by
Paul. I still love them all to this day.

Chef Henry Harris

Serves 4

Duck Tagine

Duck always turns a meal into an occasion. Flavoured with aromatic spices, this combination of rich, tender duck and root vegetables makes a splendid dinner party dish. Usefully, it can be made ahead and reheated. Serve the tagine with couscous, green beans and harissa paste for that pleasing spicy kick.

4 duck legs

salt

2 onions, chopped

1 cinnamon stick

2 tsp ground coriander

1 tsp ground ginger

1 tsp ground black pepper

800g tomatoes, grated, skins discarded

½ tsp saffron threads, soaked in 1 tbsp hot water

400ml chicken stock

200g turnips, peeled and cut into even-sized chunks

2 carrots, cut into even-sized chunks

handful of finely chopped fresh coriander

1 tbsp honey

Season the duck legs lightly with salt. Place the duck legs skin side down in a large, heavy casserole and cook over a low heat to render their fat. Once the skin is lightly golden brown, turn the legs over and cook the other side until it loses its raw look. Remove from the casserole and set aside.

Add the onion and cinnamon stick to the duck fat and fry over medium low heat for 10 minutes, stirring often, until softened. Mix in the coriander, ginger and pepper. Return the duck legs to the pan and coat with the onion mixture. Add in the grated tomatoes, saffron with its soaking water, stock, turnips and carrots. Season with salt.

Bring to the boil. Cover the casserole dish, reduce the heat to low and simmer for an hour. Check the seasoning and adjust as required. At this stage, you can cool and chill it overnight. Remove the layer of fat before you reheat it.

Stir in the fresh coriander and honey before serving.

Chicken Riesling

This all-time classic chicken dish is so simple to make. It is always worth making a little investment and using a nice Riesling wine. However, a good, dry white wine will work too. I like button mushrooms, but any firm mushroom will be just as tasty. I am partial to serving it with spaghetti, so this one is definitely going to be going all down my chin.

1 tbsp vegetable oil

40g butter

4 large chicken legs

Salt and freshly ground pepper

1 large white onion, chopped

140g pancetta, diced into lardons

4 garlic cloves, peeled

20 button mushrooms

3 sprigs of thyme

500ml Riesling wine

100ml single cream

1 egg yolk

1 tbsp chopped curly parsley

Heat ½ tbsp oil and 20g butter in a heavy bottomed pan. Season the chicken legs with salt and pepper and add them to the pan to brown. This should take about 3 minutes on each side. Remove the chicken and keep it warm.

Add the remainder of the oil and butter to the pan, then the onions and pancetta. Fry gently over a very low heat, stirring often, until the onions become translucent, but without letting them brown. Using a slotted spoon, remove the onion and pancetta and reserve. Add the mushrooms to the pan and cook for 3–4 minutes.

Remove the pan from the heat and add the chicken, onion and pancetta to the mushrooms. Add the thyme and Riesling. Return the pan to the stove and bring it to a simmer.

Simmer gently for about 30 minutes, until the chicken is cooked through and falling off of the bone. Remove the chicken with the slotted spoon and keep it warm in a serving dish.

Whisk an egg yolk into the cream and stir this into the cooking liquid. Bring it to the boil. Stir well and season to taste. Allow the liquid to simmer for 10 minutes before pouring the sauce, including the vegetables, into the serving dish, over the chicken. Sprinkle parsley over the top and serve while steaming hot. I have suggested serving with spaghetti, as it's my own favourite, but rice would be equally as nice or even a few boiled new potatoes.

Serves 4

Venison Casserole with Porcini Dumplings

Nothing says autumn like a tasty venison stew. Italian dried porcini add their wonderfully earthy flavour to this rustic dish. Root vegetables including celeriac and parsnips add a pleasant sweetness. And who doesn't love a dumpling?

700g venison shoulder, cut into 3cm cubes

2½ tbsp olive oil

1 banana shallots, finely chopped

1 celery stalk, finely sliced

1 carrot, finely diced

2 rosemary sprigs

150ml red wine

150ml port

300ml beef, game or chicken stock

½ small celeriac, cut into 2.5cm chunks

1 parsnip, chopped into 2.5cm chunks

1 garlic clove, chopped

15g dried porcini mushrooms, soaked in a little warm water for 20 minutes, soaking water strained and reserved

salt and freshly ground pepper

8 button mushrooms, halved

1 tbsp finely chopped parsley

For the porcini dumplings:
115g flour

50g suet

1 tsp porcini or cep powder

1 tbsp finely chopped parsley

salt

Preheat the oven to 180°C.

Heat 1 tbsp olive oil in a large, heavy casserole dish. Pat the venison cubes dry with kitchen paper and fry, turning as required, until browned on all sides. Remove and set aside.

Add 1 tbsp olive oil to the casserole and heat through over a low heat. Fry the shallot, celery, carrot and rosemary, stirring often, for 10 minutes. Add the browned venison with any juices to the casserole.

Pour in the red wine and port. Bring to the boil and cook vigorously, uncovered, for 5 minutes. Add in the stock, celeriac, parsnip, garlic, two-thirds of the soaked porcini and the porcini soaking water. Season with salt and pepper. Bring to the boil, skim off any scum that forms on the surface. Cover and cook in the oven for 1 hour 15 minutes.

Towards the end of this cooking time, make the porcini dumplings. Chop the remaining porcini finely. Mix together the flour, suet, porcini powder, parsley and salt. Mix in the chopped porcini. Mix in just enough cold water to form a stiff dough that holds together. Shape into 8 even-sized round dumplings.

Place the dumplings in the casserole on the surface of the stew. Cover the casserole and cook in the oven for a further 20 minutes, until the dumplings have cooked and expanded.

Heat the remaining olive oil in a little frying pan. Add in the button mushrooms and fry, stirring, until lightly browned. Add these to the casserole as a garnish, together with parsley. Serve it with wilted spinach or green beans. A little redcurrant or rowan jelly on the side would finish it off nicely.

All About the Animals

An important part of my job as a butcher is selecting good quality meat for the shops. Over the years – as someone who takes pride in what we stock – I've learnt what matters to me. The first consideration is the size and make-up – what we call the conformation – of the animal. Bones being too big create excessive wastage. Bones that are too small would signify a weaker, possibly deformed, animal. A lack of fat might mean that the animal has been poorly fed, and too much fat might mean a lack of exercise. In the butchery world we work using the EUROP scale, which indicates the ratios of fat and bone.

Different tasks call for different criteria. For example, larger, more fatty pigs for sausages where fat is needed, smaller, leaner pigs for pork chops. The next factor is 'ageing' or 'maturing' the meat. The aim of ageing is to relax the muscles for tenderisation, and allow the meat to drain excess fluids and so intensify its flavour. In red meat, a deep, ruby colour, without too much excess blood, is a good sign. Another visual indicator of high quality meat is what we know as 'marbling', that is the levels of intramuscular fat. This is important because it will let us know how well the animal has exercised and the quality of feed that it has had. The marbling effect – clear white lines of fat running through the muscles like veins – is a particularly good indicator in beef.

Soon after we opened Meat London, in 2011, I visited the abattoir in Aberdeen from where I sourced our beef. At that point, I always only bought 'Aberdeen Angus' animals. On that visit, as I was looking at the fridges, my contact, Sandy, told me that he wished I would get over the Aberdeen Angus thing. He was well aware of the specification of the animals that I wanted – the size, and the conformation. He told me that he often caught himself shaking his head as he saw cattle that would be perfect for me, but, as it was not Aberdeen Angus, he couldn't send. It was a revelation. I realised that I never restricted myself to breeds of other animals, so why was I restricting myself to one breed of beef, which was invariably crossed anyway? All I really wanted was the best meat that Sandy could send. We shook hands there and then and my obsession with Aberdeen Angus ended. I will caveat that by noting that Aberdeen Angus is still some of the finest beef in the world.

So, what do I look for in the animals that we use? Well, I remember watching Albert Roux on TV in the 1980s, talking to fellow chefs. He said that lambs should be running and playing in the fields. A 'happy' lamb will taste the best he declared. There was a small, derogatory snigger around the table. Chef Albert was ahead of his time. It would be another 10–15 years before the restaurant industry would take a serious interest in the lives the animals led and the importance of free-range, high welfare animals. By the time I started selecting meat for the Harvey Nichols Foodmarket in 1992, I was beginning to appreciate of the benefits of good husbandry.

Exploring this option meant that at every turn I came across bright, enthusiastic farmers. They explained how and why they reared their animals, with the breed of the animal rarely being the big story. I met the delightful Helen Browning of Eastbrook Farm, who was in the process of converting Eastbrook into a fully organic farm. She would go on to head the Soil Association and become an enthusiastic champion of organic

food in Britain. Hampshire farmer Sam Olive produced superb pork by crossing wild boar with domestic breeds, creating a wonderful fat covering that the chefs loved. As my first Christmas at Harvey Nichols came up, Howard Blackwell approached me with his fully free-range turkeys and geese. I still work with Howard today.

As a butcher, I have spent my working life talking to producers to understand how and why they do what they do and visiting their farms to see for myself the conditions the animals are reared in. It is not an accident that most of the farmers and producers that I work with have become good acquaintances, or even good friends. We all have so much in common.

Just like people, livestock need an active, outdoor life, with fresh air and exercise, a balanced natural diet, fresh and wholesome foods, and rest and relaxation. The best animals live on the land. They get their exercise and rest when they feel the need. They roam and wander and look for natural

feed. Of course, in inclement weather, or in winter months, animals may be brought into barns for their comfort, and they would then be fed on hay or natural silage. In contrast to intensively farmed animals, these are slow growing animals, taking time to develop muscle, bones and intra-muscular fat, thus creating flavour.

Of course, having given an animal a good life, and having ensured that they have been cared for, it then becomes equally as important to make sure that they are well treated at slaughter. As a buyer and a retailer, this is an important part of the process when it comes to eating quality. Animals going to slaughter need to be relaxed and calm. A frightened animal will suffer a surge of adrenalin, and a surge of blood could discolour the meat and, potentially, adversely affect flavour and texture. Abattoirs use any number of methods to relax the animals, including music and darkened rooms. Abattoirs are controlled by Government food standard agencies and have to have

a vet on site. Although it seems a strange consideration at the point of kill, the animal's welfare is the key consideration throughout the process. The general standards of British abattoirs is very high. The ones I've visited have always been meticulously clean. When in full swing, everything moves fast and with precision. The men and women who work in abattoirs are expert in what they do. They know their task and work skilfully, with respect for the animals that they slaughter. It's important to appreciate the importance that good abattoirs have in the food chain.

Once the carcasses arrive at the shops, it becomes the butcher's responsibility to use their skills to prepare them well. There is little point in the farmers having worked so hard to give the animals a good life, if we don't then do them justice at the butchering stage. For many reasons, practical and ethical, it is important to use as much of the animal as possible. The idea of 'nose to tail' eating is a growing mantra and is one embraced through the butcher's shop. We offer our customers

lamb shanks, pig's feet, beef or pig's cheek, offal including chicken livers, sweetbreads and kidneys and bones for stock. Even the delicious pork ribs are by-product.

Profit is obviously a consideration, but so, too, is the important need to avoid food waste. The skills that a good butcher offers are considerable. Cutting the bone in the wrong place, slashing through a muscle, trimming off too much or too little fat or sinew will affect the meat and reduce profits. While a diligent novice butcher can make themselves part of the team within a few months of good training, it takes years to perfect the art. Without doubt, one of the greatest compliments a butcher cutting meat will receive is when a customer comments "it looks so easy". In a busy environment, with customers waiting to be served, knowing how to prepare the desired cut, knowing where the bones lie or how the seams join the muscles is key to doing the best possible job. The best butcher will be judged by the waste bin. An empty bin reflects a good day.

PLEASE
DO NOT FEED
THE PIGS

BASICS

Taking Stock

As a butcher, it's very frustrating, when people come into the shop and ask for 'left overs' or 'something that is to be thrown away', for the dog. If butchers left enough meat on the bone to feed the average dog, we wouldn't be in business for very long. Likewise with trimmings of fat and gristle. Now, I must confess, that I fall into the category of the general public who can never find the 'leftover wine', that so many recipes call for. I subscribe to using up everything I pay for. To my mind, 'You can eat all of the pig except it's oink' should be a mantra for the whole food industry – and imprinted on the mind of every chef, retailer or domestic cook. It's the right thing to do morally, ethically and financially.

I'm writing this book to offer an insight into which meat cuts should be used for which dishes, so it's impossible not to conclude without touching on bones for stock.

The importance of stock in the kitchen is something that I learnt about as a chef. In the classic French kitchen there are two fundamental types of meat stocks: brown and white. A brown stock is made using the roasted bones from red meat animals, so beef and lamb. Bones that contain bone marrow are the great secret ingredient when it comes to brown stock, as this gives a rich, full flavour. White stock is made from poultry bones, so chicken and turkey. Game birds, duck or goose carcasses can also be used, with the stock they make being darker in colour. Home-made stock has a wonderful depth of flavour and is essential not just for soups but also sauces. Make a batch of stock and store it in your freezer and you will see for yourself just how useful and versatile it is.

Stocks must not boil!"

Making a stock is simple. There are a few basic rules to follow:

First rule – use good bones
A decent butcher can help here.

Second rule – STOCKS MUST NOT BOIL!
Even at 60 years of age, I can clearly hear Head Chef Chris Oakley constantly shouting the instruction at my 17-year- old self, while learning my trade at the Michelin- starred Le Poulbot Restaurant. If a stock boils, it goes cloudy, which is a cardinal sin in a professional kitchen. For a white stock the bones should be clean and un-cooked, and vegetables should be peeled and clean of any blemish. Brown stocks are the opposite. Here the bones and vegetables are cut into small pieces to create more surface area to colour and impart flavour. These are roasted until they are golden brown. Some chefs suggest frying rather than roasting, but this is much messier, so stick to the oven.

Third rule – add aromatics to the stock
A bouquet garni is a way of infusing your stock with the flavours of wonderful garden herbs without throwing the whole bunch into your stock. Simply wrap a few thyme stems, sage leaves, curly parsley and a little oregano in a large bay leaf and tie the bunch of herbs together with string.

**Makes approx
1 litre**

White Stock

2 raw chicken carcasses

2 litres fresh, cold water

1 large onion, peeled

1 large carrot, peeled

2 celery stalks

1 bouquet garni

Choose a stock pot that is large enough to submerge the bones entirely. Put the carcasses into the pot and cover with the water. Heat the water until just before boiling point (just as the water starts to move). A scum will form on the surface. Skim this off carefully with a spoon. Now add the vegetables and bouquet garni and top the stock pot up again with fresh, cold water. Return to the stove and let the stock simmer for about two to three hours. The liquid will reduce by about half.

Remove from the stove and let the liquid settle. After a minute or two, pour the stock through a fine sieve. It's even better if you can line the sieve with some muslin (an old, clean pair of tights will do the trick too). Pour gently, not too fast. Once the stock has settled, you will have a clear, rich base, full of flavour, from which to make your white sauces or soups.

Brown Stock

2kg beef, veal, lamb or game
    bones, chopped into small
    pieces (ask your helpful
    butcher to do this for you)

1 large onion, chopped

2 large tomatoes, halved

2 carrots, medium diced

2 celery stalks, medium diced

1 whole garlic bulb

5 litres fresh cold water

Preheat the oven to 220°C. Place the bones, onion, tomatoes, carrots, celery and garlic in a large roasting tin or two smaller ones. Roast in the oven until everything is golden brown, between 30-45 minutes. Every ten minutes carefully turn and mix everything.

Remove from the oven and put all of the roasted bones and the vegetables into a stock pot. Be sure to scrape in the juices and sediment from the bottom of the roasting pan. Add in the water and bring to the simmer. Skim off any scum that forms on the surface and reduce the heat to the lowest level possible. The liquid should be barely moving. The water will evaporate slowly and gently, which will concentrate the flavour of the stock.

Simmer the stock for at least four or five hours or longer if possible. Check it every 30 minutes and skim off any scum that rises to the surface. When the liquid has reduced by about one third, remove from the stove and let it settle for a few minutes. The stock should now be treated gently. The bottom of the cooking pot will be full of sediment and 'debris' that you don't want to mix back through your stock.

Remove as many of the bones as possible from the pot. Use a ladle to pour the stock through a fine sieve, again using muslin. Let the stock cool, then chill in the fridge where it will keep for two days, or place in containers and freeze. Remember that liquid expands when frozen so

don't overfill the containers. Another tiny tip, many sauces ask for a little stock to be added. Freezing stock in an ice cube tray will ensure that you always have a small portion of stock to hand if you need it.

Of course, simply by altering the amount of ingredients, you can make more or less. The size of your pot will probably determine the volume that you can make.

Now you will have a great stock, which is the basis of fabulous sauces and soups. Making your own stock is an investment of time that really pays off when you use it in cooking.

Remouillage – Second stock or 're-boil from the French word meaning 're-wetting'.

As you know, at Meat London we're all about making the most of your ingredients. Here is the final opportunity for thrifty cooking when it comes to making stock.

Having made your first stock, which is ideal for sauces, stews or soups, you can use the remaining stock ingredients again. Place the bones and flavourings in a large, clean pot, top up with fresh water, bring to boiling point, reduce the heat and simmer for two hours. The results will be weaker than the first, prime stock, but one that can be put to good use in soups or poached dishes or reduced to intensify its flavour.

Another tip is not to throw away the bones of roasted lamb or beef or poultry or game carcases, but instead use them to make stock. Place them in a pot with onion, tomatoes, carrots, celery and garlic and parsley, cover with fresh water, bring to boiling point, reduce the heat and simmer for 2 hours, then strain and use or freeze as needed.

Once you've conjured up a remouillage, you can sit back, confident in the knowledge that you really have extricated every ounce of goodness from those bones you bought.

Normandy French Onion Soup

Homemade soups are so delicious and such a treat to come home to on a cold, blustery evening or to share with friends over lunch. Once you have made a sturdy stock, a soup is generally quite quick to make, and you can be sitting down to something hearty and warming within an hour. One of my favourites is French onion soup and here I have put a Normandy slant on it by adding, what I believe to be, some of the world's finest cider. The other thing to note about the Normandy version is that it calls for chicken stock, whereas most onion soups call for beef stock.

100g butter

400g white onions, thinly sliced

Salt and freshly ground black pepper

250ml dry cider (Normandy cider would be best, but use what you can find)

30g plain flour

650ml chicken stock

12 slices of French baguette. about 1cm thick

30g grated Gruyere cheese

70ml double cream

Melt 70g butter in a heavy bottomed pot. Just as the butter starts to foam, add the onions and fry them gently until they take on a golden colour, about 4–6 minutes. Season them with pepper and a little salt. Carry on cooking, stirring often, until the onions are brown. Take care not to let them burn! Once they are brown, add 150ml (about two-thirds) of the cider and stir well. Bring to a boil and allow to cook for 2 minutes before removing from the heat.

In a separate pot, melt the remaining butter and add the flour to make a roux. Cook out the roux for 1 minute before gradually whisking in the chicken stock. Let the thickened mixture cook for a further 2 minutes and then add in the cooked onion and cider mixture. Simmer for a further 10 minutes so that all of the delicious flavours combine.

Meanwhile, toast the baguette slices on both sides and share the remaining cider between 4 soup bowls. Ladle a good helping of the onion soup into each soup bowl and place the baguette on top of each. Liberally sprinkle the Gruyere on to the baguette and a splash of double cream. Put the soup under the grill to make the cheese melt – or do use a blow torch if you have one. Serve while the cheese is still bubbling.

A Bit on the Side

How often do we say, "serve with a chunk of crusty bread"? Bread goes so well with comforting soups, tasty pâtés and terrines, our wonderful British cheeses and is essential for a 'doorstep' rare roast beef sandwich. And then, what about other accompaniments – delicious chips, a dollop of coleslaw?

You might be asking yourself "why is Paul including a bread recipe in his Meat London cookbook?" Well, it won't do any harm to give over a few pages to a few useful and delicious accompaniments. Let's take five minutes away from the meat!

Crusty Bread

Bread making is so much fun, so relaxing and really easy. It does need a little time, but mostly waiting for the dough to rise, or 'prove'. The ingredients are few and simple, and it takes only minutes to mix them together and give the dough a good knead before letting them prove while you're having your pre-breakfast shower. Ok, maybe I'm over-egging things, but I'm sure you get my point. The end result of having your own, home-made, warm bread far outweighs the effort that goes into it. Bread is one of those things that you can get a bit obsessive about. Once you get into making your own bread, you'll never stop, and the options are many: white bread, brown bread, wholegrain bread, sourdough breads, focaccia, rye bread. Here's a simple crusty bread recipe to get you started. You're going to thank me for this!

5oog strong, white flour

1 tsp salt

40g butter, softened

1 pkt (6g) fast action yeast

300ml water (using lukewarm water will help activate the yeast, but it's not crucial)

Put the flour, salt and butter into a large bowl and mix together. Add the dried yeast and mix again. Make a well in the middle of the flour and slowly add about two-thirds of the water. Draw the flour back into the middle and start mixing the dough. Once loosely mixed, add the remaining water and mix thoroughly until the dough starts to leave the sides of the bowl.

Turn out onto a lightly floured surface. Knead the dough for between 5–10 minutes until it is smooth and slightly elastic. Form into a ball, return to the bowl and cover with a cloth or cling film. Leave to rest for 2 hours at room temperature.

Turn the dough back onto the floured surface and re-form into a ball. Place your ball onto a baking sheet and rest for another hour, during which time the dough should rise to form a beautiful dome. Make a slash across the top of the dough and dust with flour.

During the final resting stage, preheat the oven to 220˚C. Bake the loaf in the oven for 30 minutes until golden brown. When your bread is cooked, it will be crusty and crispy on the outside; if the top feels soft, the bread is likely not quite cooked. A fun way to check is to turn your bread upside down and give a firm tap on the bottom. A bit like hitting a drum. If you hear a good, hollow sound, your bread is done. Let your loaf cool on a wire rack.

Simple Chips

Steak and chips, burger and chips... there is something irresistible about these deep-fried pieces of potato. Chefs go on about triple-cooked chips, but listen, lean in – and for goodness sake don't tell any chefs – when you're short of time, this is a great simple way to make delicious chips.

What you do need is a good, chipping potato. Maris Piper and King Edwards are widely available and work a treat. I peel my potatoes for chips – I think it's so lazy to leave the skin on. Cut your chips into 1cm-thick fingers. The length is not so important, but remember they do have to fit into your pan. Rinse in cold water to wash off the starch, as this stops them sticking together, then roll well in a clean cloth to remove any excess water. Tip the chips into a deep, heavy bottomed pan. Pour in cooking oil – vegetable or sunflower – until all the potatoes are well covered. Heat the oil until it gradually comes to a vigorous simmer.

As the oil starts to heat up, it will blanch the potatoes. About 10 minutes into the cooking give the pan a careful shake (remember the oil is hot) or stir the chips gently to stop them sticking. By 15 minutes you will be up to a full simmer and the chips will start to crisp and colour. At about 25 mins, you will have near perfect chips.

Remove from the heat and using a slotted spoon transfer the chips from the oil onto a piece of kitchen paper to drain. Place the hot chips in a deep bowl and salt immediately. Toss well and serve the chips while they're piping hot.

I love chips – especially with a good, rich, mustard mayonnaise (see p.79).

> I'm not sure if chips were invented for mayonnaise, or mayonnaise was invented for chips, but it is a heavenly combination.

Coleslaw

Home-made coleslaw is so simple and fresh and goes so well with so many dishes. When it comes to making it, pretty much any fresh, crunchy vegetable works well. The key is to slice or grate everything as thinly as possible and look for a vibrant mix of colours and flavours.

¼ white cabbage

¼ red cabbage

½ white onion

1 large carrot, peeled

½ tsp celery salt

½ tsp freshly ground black pepper

2 tsp mint leaves, finely sliced

3 tbsp mayonnaise (see p.79)

1 tbsp lemon juice

If you have a sharp knife, and enough confidence, remove the core from the white and red cabbage and slice both as thinly as possible. Thinly slice the onion, too. Best though to grate the carrot with a grater. If your kitchen aid has a grating attachment, you could use that. Just don't tell me.

Put the sliced vegetables in a large bowl with the celery salt, black pepper and mint leaves and mix well.

In a separate bowl, mix together the mayonnaise and lemon juice. Add it to the vegetable bowl. Give everything a really good mix by lifting and dropping. Try not to squeeze and bruise your vegetables. Transfer your coleslaw into a nice serving bowl and job done. It will keep for two days covered in the fridge.

Serves 6–8

Gratin Dauphinoise

Another great accompaniment. So simple to put together and very difficult to get wrong. Piles of floury baking potatoes seasoned with garlic, thyme, nutmeg and pepper and all brought together with thick cream. Back in the early 00's, when I owned The Butcher & Grill, our Chef, David Massey, made the best Gratin Dauphinoise ever, and I was quite happy to have just that for lunch. Now, for those seeking pure opulence, this can be made with just cream, but it also suits 50/50, or any combination actually, with milk. Mix the two together at the boiling stage. A good handful of grated Gruyere on top and – oh boy!

1kg baking potatoes (King Edwards or Desiree)

2 garlic cloves, crushed

1 tsp chopped thyme leaves or ½ tsp dried thyme

¼ tsp grated nutmeg

Salt and freshly ground pepper

500ml double cream or half and half with full cream milk

1 garlic clove, peeled and cut in half

30g butter

50g Gruyere cheese, grated

Peel the potatoes and slice them to about 3mm. This is best done on a mandolin. Lay the potatoes on a clean cloth and pat them dry.

Put the potato slices in a large bowl. Add in the crushed garlic, thyme and nutmeg, and season well with salt and pepper. Mix everything thoroughly without breaking the potato slices

Pour the cream, and milk if you are using it, into a saucepan and bring to boiling point. Turn the heat off as soon as the liquid comes to the boil. Pour it into the mixing bowl with the potatoes and mix well.

When it comes to baking the gratin you need dish 4–6cm deep, large enough to take all of the potatoes and cream. An oblong dish of 30cm x 20cm is about right.

Rub the two halves of garlic all around the inside of the dish and then spread the butter around the dish as well. Start to spread the potato mix around the dish. Building up the layers as you go. It doesn't need to look pretty on the first couple of layers but try to get the potato spread evenly. Keep some of the larger, more even pieces of potato for the top layer for presentation purposes. Pour over any remaining cream from the bowl. Sprinkle over the grated Gruyere.

Preheat the oven to 180°C. Cover the dish with foil and put it into the centre of the oven for 1 hour. After the hour, remove the foil from the gratin and bake in the oven for a further 30 minutes until golden brown. When the gratin dauphinoise is fully cooked, a sharp knife will go straight through without resistance.

Rough Puff Pastry

This is not difficult, but it does take time and patience. However, the rewards are worth the effort. Apart from the pleasure of having done it yourself, you will have an all butter puff pastry that will rise beautifully and taste amazing. I'm going to explain a little about rolling and folding the pastry, but most home cooks will have heard about 'turns in three' and 'book turns'. It is this turning that creates the many layers that, in turn, create the beautiful, light rise of the pastry. Every pastry making recipe will always tell you to keep all of the ingredients, and the necessary tools, as cold as possible. This is to stop the butter melting so very important to remember.

250g plain flour

150g cold butter, cut into very small pieces.

100ml ice cold water

Put the flour into a good sized bowl and add the butter. Rub the butter into the flour until it is well broken down. You don't need to achieve the breadcrumb effect of short crust pastry, and you don't want the butter getting warm from your hands.

Add in the water 3 tbsp at a time, and mix to create a dough. Add more water, a little at a time, until your dough holds together. You may not need to use all of the water. Tip the contents of the bowl onto a clean surface and form the dough into an oblong shape. Wrap the dough in cling film and chill in the fridge for 10 minutes.

Remove the dough from the fridge, and bring it back to your lightly floured work surface. With a rolling pin, roll the pastry into an oblong shape, away from you, to about 30cm x 20cm. Now, fold the first third of the pastry onto the second third, and bring the final third back onto the second. This is called a 'turn in three'.

Turn your dough around so that the seam is on one side. Now roll your dough back into it's 30cm x 20cm oblong. This time, fold the first quarter of the dough into the middle of your oblong and the fourth quarter, back towards you, also into the middle. Now you should be able to fold the two sides together like a book. This is called a 'book turn'.

Put your pastry back into the fridge for 20 minutes. You will need to do this process four more times at 20 minutes intervals. When you have finished the folding process, put the pastry into the fridge for 30 minutes before using it. The pastry will last for up to three days in the fridge.

Thank you for reading the Meat London Book

As already mentioned, I have been working in the food and hospitality industry for a very long time. I am on record, probably far too often, as saying that I have enjoyed every minute of it, and I really couldn't think what else I would have done with my working life. It has been great.

Along the way, I have seen fantastic product. I have witnessed the production of most food types and I have met amazing people, doing extraordinary things. It has been my good fortune to spend time in Europe, visiting producers who have all treated me well and entertained me to a level that would not always be appropriate on these pages! I could write a book about just that, but that is not the purpose of this book.

I have wanted to share with you, the reader, some of my experiences. I wanted to give an insight into what goes on out the back of the shop and I wanted to give guidance on which meat to use at which time, for which purpose. Through this book I wanted to encourage you to see food and food production in a positive light. I wanted you to understand why the best products cost a little more, and why the extra is worth paying. I hope I have been able to instil confidence in being able to demand (politely request) more from your local butcher and I hope to have filled you with enthusiasm to try something new.

If only I was super-human, I could have done it all on my own. Alas, I'm not, but I have been lucky to have been surrounded by wonderful people who have shared my vision and enthusiasm. Mum and Dad set me on the right course, and my two sisters, Bernadine and Jacqueline helped me live a fantastic childhood. Of course, professionally, it all started with the Roux Family, and my gratitude for what they gave me is unlimited. For over more than 40 years I have worked with employers and colleagues who have encouraged me, taught me and laughed with me.

In the last 10 years, at Meat London, we have employed dozens of people who have made the business a success. I couldn't start to name them all, but they know who they are. Marc Wise and Richard Jocelyn had the vision to see that N16 needed a butcher's shop, and they made it happen. Marc moved on to other ventures, but Richard is still here, as my partner. Chis Wood and Jason Walduck came on board as Directors and Shareholders. I would mention Troy Dickerson, Ryan McKernan, Michael McGrath, Sam Mitchell and Gessica Di Giovanni as the team that got it all started, and remain committed today.

How does one thank the hundreds of customers and suppliers, without whom there can be no business? I am not sure, but 'Thank You' to all.

This book is the culmination of so much of what I have achieved, and, as I think about it, there are five ladies who have made it all possible.

Agata Klus came from Poland in 2006, and joined a previous company that I owned, before I asked her to take on Meat London, as General Manager. Agata helped guide the business from a start-up to the success it is today. Agata was by my side for 14 years and is a good friend. I was introduced to Lesley Gilmour, who has been responsible for expressing my ideas and writing through the beautiful design of the book. Caroline Mardon is the vegetarian photographer who I have made traipse across muddy farms, and who has turned the working lives of our Team and our meat into glorious print. Caroline has been funny and relaxed throughout. Jenny Linford needs no introduction to the world of food writing. How lucky have I been that Jenny agreed to take on this project? She has tutored me, cajoled me, encouraged at every turn and Jenny has 'held my hand' throughout. Such a lovely lady and, once again, I have been so lucky to have been able to work with the very best.

Finally, I have an amazing wife. We both work in the food industry and we understand how it works. We will have been married for 25 years in 2021. I work hard and long hours, I can be stubborn and grumpy and I drink too much wine. It frustrates her that I fall asleep during Match of the Day, and I can't name the birds that land on our bird table. However, I do cook for her, and I am capable with the iron. What more could a girl ask for? Sue calms me down, she is a positive influence and tolerates my madcap ideas with patience and support. As much as I would like to deny it, Sue proves the old adage that 'behind every good man, there is a better woman'.

Paul Grout

Index

A

Abattoirs 257
A Day in the Life of Meat London 128
All About the Animals 257, 259
Anchovy Butter 39
Au Poivre 31

B

Bacon 40, 41, 52, 72, 163, 172, 239
Baking 137, 271, 276
Balls, Ed *vii*
Barbecues:
    Charcoal 88, 91, 93, 100, 107, 130, 138, 167
    Direct & indirect heat 91, 97, 109, 118, 121, 167
    How to light 88
Barbecuing 87-127:
    Beef 92-97
    Lamb 98-105
    Pork 106-110, 115-121
    Poultry and Game 122-
Barnsley Chops with Garden Herbs 49
Basics 263-277
Bearnaise Sauce 30-32
Fillet, beef 35, 216
Beef *214-17:*
    Argentinian Chorizo Sausage Rolls 172
    Barbecuing 92-97
    Beef essay 214-17
    Beef, Mushroom & Red Pepper Stir-fry 29
    Beef Satay with Peanut Dipping Sauce 94
    Beef Shin a l'Ancienne 211
    Breeds 227
    Brisket 91,139, 217
    Brown stock 266-67
    Burgers, 72, 75
    Chinese Ox Cheek Casserole 210
    Chuck 36, 172, 202, 208, 217, 219-20
    Clod 217
    Daube de Boeuf 208-9
    Fillet 35, 216
    Korean Chilli Beef Short Ribs 93
    Onglet Steak with Sauce Bordelaise 26

Ox Tail Ragu 221
    Rare Roast Beef Topside 144
    Roast Beef Forerib with Marrow Bone Gravy 141-42
    Rump 29, 32, 36, 94, 216
    Shin 200, 202, 211, 217
    Six hour Ox Cheeks 97
    Steak and Kidney Pie 219-20
    Steaks 25, 26, 29, 30, 31, 32-36
    Thai Steak Salad 25
    See also Veal
Beef Chilli Burger 75
Beef, Mushroom and Red Pepper Stir-fry 29
Beef Satay with Peanut Dipping Sauce 94
Beef Shin a L'Ancienne 211
Bibendum 5, 186
Black pudding 40, 41
Blanquette de Veau (Veal Blanquette) 205
Braised Kimchi Meatballs 241
Braised Lamb Shanks 233
Braising 200, 233, 241
Braising, Stewing & Poaching 199-255:
    Beef 204-211, 219-225
    Lamb 232-37
    Pork 238-241
    Poultry & Game 246-48, 252-55
Bread 271
Bread Sauce 184, 185
Breakfast 40-43
    Full English Breakfast 40
Brown Stock 266-67
Burgers 66, 72, 74, 91, 208, 217:
    Beef Chili Burger 75
    Chicken and Herb Burger 75
    Lamb and Mint Burger 75
    Pork and Apple Burger 75
Burger Sauces and relishes 76
Butcher's *vii*, 13-16, 258-59
Butcher's Essay 13-16
Butchery 4, 6, 8, 13-16, 67, 132, 133, 228, 242, 257

C

Cassoulet 239
Charcuterie 5, 7, 115, 239
Chicken 244-45:
    Chicken and Herb Burger 75

MEAT N16
BUTCHER & DELICATESSEN
MEAT N16
BUTCHER & DELICATESSEN
www.meatlondon.co.uk

Published in 2021 by Cloke Press

Recipes & text by Paul Grout
Photography & prop styling by Caroline Mardon
Food styling by Caroline Mardon and Craig Martin
Edited by Jenny Linford
Book design by Lesley Gilmour
Cover illustration by Lara Christie

Printed and bound in Italy by L.E.G.O.

British Library Cataloguing in Publication Data. A catalogue record for
this book is available from the British Library.

ISBN 978-1-9168747-0-1